# THE
# POWER
## OF THE
# PIVOT

## A Strategic Guide to Aligning
## Action with Vision in Business

### ALISHA AND MAURICE
# PENNINGTON

THE POWER OF THE PIVOT

A STRATEGIC GUIDE TO ALIGNING ACTION WITH VISION IN BUSINESS

ALISHA AND MAURICE PENNINGTON

For more information: connect@p10.co

ISBN Paperback: 978-1-962280-71-6

ISBN eBook: 978-1-962280-72-3

To our daughters, Tatum and Sloan, who remind us every day of why alignment matters. May you always pursue your dreams with purpose and courage. And to those who dare to live with intention and take bold, aligned action—may this book be the spark that ignites your journey toward a life you're proud of. We believe in you.

# TABLE OF CONTENTS

# INTRODUCTION

It's the summer of 2014 in Anaheim, California. We're staring at yet another rent adjustment letter from our apartment manager. By now, we've come to expect these—the result of five years spent chasing move-in specials because we've never been able to afford the inevitable rent hikes.

But this time, something is different. Alisha has started her own fully remote staffing company, and it's doing well. Maurice is graduating from college in less than a year. Now, the decision of what we do next doesn't hinge on staying in Anaheim—or even in California.

Still, everything we know is rooted in California. We grew up here—our friends, our professional networks, and our business are all here. We've even been trying to buy a house. It's been our dream to stay in California; it's where we were raised and where we love to be. California is part of our identity.

Yet every time we visit Alisha's parents in Arizona, we never want to leave. It's cleaner. Less congested. Even peaceful. And really, when we think about it, we don't have to stay in California—people could come visit us in Arizona. That could be a fun way to stay connected to friends, hosting them in our home. Oh, a home! There, we could afford a beautiful house and live comfortably instead of being stuck in an apartment with constantly increasing rent. Actually, relocating could get us ahead, help us build equity, and give us a real shot at financial independence. That sounds magical.

Wait, but what about our careers? What would moving mean for the business we've worked so hard to build? It's still so new, just a few years old and only really gaining momentum. And what about Maurice's career in broadcast journalism? He hasn't even graduated yet and we're already thinking of going to another state? Would we make any friends in a new state? Oh, wait, and how would it feel to no longer identify as Californians? We have so much of our identity tied up in being from this state.

The back-and-forth between what life "could be" in Arizona and the life we'd be giving up in California was paralyzing. Versions of this conversation went on for months. Inevitably, the decision boiled down to two crucial questions: What do we really want? And why are we doing this?

We eventually realized that what we wanted was simple: to invest in real estate, have autonomy over our time, and be able to travel.

And why were we doing this? We were about to become newlyweds and start our life together. We wanted the foundation of our marriage to reflect stability and forward growth.

Once we got to the answer of these questions, we knew we couldn't stay in California. It was a hard truth, but if we were serious about the vision we had for ourselves, we knew what the right decision was. We had to remove the things that didn't actually matter. It wasn't about our friends or the identity we'd built there. It was our ego that wanted us to stay in CA. And our emotions that wanted our friends to be physically close to us. But we made the difficult choice because relocating aligned with the life we wanted. We understood that new challenges would inevitably arise, but we believed that staying true to ourselves would ultimately serve us, which in turn would serve our clients and our business and our careers best. By taking aligned action with our vision, we trusted that solutions would present themselves, even when we couldn't yet see them.

Our friends questioned us. We kept it quiet from all business clients, and our families wondered if we would be happy. From the outside, it seemed like a rash decision that did not align with how we had been living our lives. But the truth was, the way we had been living—hopping from apartment to apartment and chasing a life in California—was what had been out of alignment. Moving to another state where we could have stability, begin investing in real estate, and run our business remotely was the true alignment we had been seeking in our pursuit of degrees and business ownership over the previous several years.

Fast-forward: We've now been in business for over a decade. We've grown from earning four figures in our first year to consistent seven-figure revenues. We've kept a core staff of the managerial personnel for those same ten-plus years. We've made the Inc. 5000 list for three consecutive years.

We've mentored hundreds of businesses and leaders. We've bought and sold five houses, flipping them to increase equity. We even built our custom home from scratch and own several investment properties. In short, it was the right decision. Even with all we've achieved, we still come back to those same essential questions whenever decisions or opportunities arise.

In reflecting on our journey, here's what we've learned:

- Every decision comes back to our why.
- There are no losses—only lessons to grow from.
- We thrive on adaptability and resilience in the face of change.

We assess, we act, we evaluate, we adjust. It's a series of pivots, again and again. There is no final destination. That is what has brought us to where we are today.

Is there something unique about us? Special even? Only in that our success can be attributed to having a proactive mindset and taking aligned action. By continually assessing and adjusting, we remain ready to face new challenges and seize opportunities. This approach hasn't just driven our personal and professional growth—it's embedded a culture of continuous improvement in our businesses and the businesses we consult with.

Unfortunately, the reality for most people, in both life and business, is that they are so busy reacting that they don't have time to proactively take aligned action. In fact, they often don't even realize that aligned action is an option. Life is consistently happening to them, and they must react to as much as possible in order to survive.

If that sounds familiar, you are not alone. This was us, hopping from apartment to apartment in Anaheim. We reacted to the new rent increase letter we received every year. In fact, we braced ourselves for it, anticipating what the increase might be, shopping around for new options knowing it was coming. We were constantly affected by the market conditions. What we found was this reactive mode wasn't just limited to our circumstances; it is the default programming in most businesses and leaders we consult with too. It wasn't until we identified the aforementioned crucial questions, and more specifically the question of "why are we doing this," that we began to find answers within ourselves.

→ **We assess, we act, we evaluate, we adjust. It's a series of pivots, again and again. There is no final destination.**

Simon Sinek's *Start with Why* explores this concept in depth, emphasizing the importance of understanding the fundamental purpose that drives our actions. Sinek argues that successful individuals and organizations are rooted in a clear sense of purpose—their "why"—which serves as a guiding principle for decision-making and long-term success. This framework helps ensure that actions are aligned with core values, allowing for greater impact and more meaningful outcomes. Sinek's work shows that having a clear why isn't just a philosophical exercise—it's a practical approach that leads to extraordinary outcomes[1].

Without a clear sense of purpose or "why," many leaders remain stuck in reactive mode, focusing solely on maintaining the status quo and ensuring survival.

In other words, they are constantly playing defense.

---

[1] Simon Sinek, *Start with Why: How Great Leaders Inspire Everyone to Take Action* (Harlow, England: Penguin Publishing Group, 2011).

We've all heard the saying, "Defense wins championships," which highlights the importance of reactivity and the benefits it brings. But what purpose does defense serve if it doesn't transition into offense?

For us, that realization was key. We had developed a strong skill set in responding to crises and managing challenges as they came, but we soon realized that constantly playing defense wasn't going to get us where we wanted to be. We were ready to move beyond survival mode and shift toward actively creating the future we envisioned. We wanted more than just managing the present—we wanted to build something greater.

Some of the greatest coaches in American sports history understood that transitioning from a defensive, reactive posture to a proactive, offensive one was essential for long-term success.

## TURNING DEFENSE INTO OFFENSE

Pat Summitt, the legendary coach of the University of Tennessee Lady Volunteers, epitomized turning defense into offense. Known for her aggressive defensive tactics, Summitt's teams were relentless in applying pressure, forcing turnovers, and securing defensive rebounds. But these defensive efforts were not just about preventing the opponent from scoring; they were the foundation for her offensive strategy. Summitt trained her players to transition swiftly from defense to a fast-break offense, capitalizing on the chaos created by their defensive stops. This seamless shift caught opponents off guard, leading to easy scoring opportunities and a constant offensive threat.

Renowned for his defensive acumen, Bill Belichick, the

former head coach of the New England Patriots, further exemplifies the art of turning defense into offense. His teams excelled at forcing turnovers through strategic game planning and in-game adjustments. By focusing on defensive strategies—such as pressuring the quarterback, disguising coverages, and executing timely blitzes—Belichick created opportunities for his team to regain possession.

→ **A company that can pivot from a defensive posture (such as managing risks and stabilizing operations) to an offensive strategy (anticipating changes, seizing opportunities, and driving innovation) can transform from merely surviving to actively thriving.**

Once the ball was back in their hands, the Patriots capitalized on the momentum shift. Belichick's offensive philosophy is built on exploiting the weaknesses of opponents' defenses, often leading to quick scores and altering the game's dynamics. This seamless transition from defense to offense not only disrupts the opponent's rhythm but also keeps them constantly on the back foot, unable to predict the next move.

Gregg Popovich, head coach of the San Antonio Spurs, has built a dynasty on the principle of using disciplined defense to set up efficient offense. Popovich's teams are known for developing strong defensive schemes by focusing on sound fundamentals, communication, and teamwork. This defensive discipline often results in forced turnovers and missed shots by opponents.

After regaining control of possession, Popovich's Spurs excel in transition, moving the ball quickly and efficiently to find the best scoring opportunities. The team's offensive success is directly tied to their defensive prowess, as they convert defensive stops into well-executed offensive plays, maintaining a high level of efficiency and control over the game.

The lessons from Pat Summitt, Bill Belichick, and Gregg Popovich underscore the importance of not remaining on the defensive but turning that defense into offense. In business, this means not just reacting to market challenges but leveraging them to create new opportunities. A company that can pivot from a defensive posture (such as managing risks and stabilizing operations) to an offensive strategy (anticipating changes, seizing opportunities, and driving innovation) can transform from merely surviving to actively thriving. This is exactly what we enabled for ourselves when we decided to leave California. We transitioned from surviving to thriving, both personally and professionally.

## THE PIVOT FRAMEWORK

This book provides the opportunity to shift from merely reacting to events to taking a more deliberate, forward-thinking approach. It's a strategy that equips you to anticipate changes in the marketplace, identify emerging opportunities, and reorient your strategies to align more directly with your vision. We call it the PIVOT framework.

For us, the PIVOT framework emerged out of necessity. That pivotal decision back in 2014 set the foundation for how we approach decision-making and problem-solving today. Whether Maurice is designing a home for our family or others or Alisha is developing scalable strategies for a business, the PIVOT framework guides our every move. It has not only shaped our business but also provided clarity and direction for countless entrepreneurs we've mentored. This framework is more than a tool—it's a way of thinking, a way of navigating both personal and professional challenges with purpose and intention.

## Using the PIVOT framework enables you to adopt a proactive stance by setting the agenda rather than reacting to it.

Using the PIVOT framework enables you to adopt a proactive stance by setting the agenda rather than reacting to it. It involves making aligned decisions that not only safeguard the business but also position it for growth and competitive advantage. Just as Summitt, Belichick, and Popovich used defense to fuel their offensive success, companies can turn challenges into catalysts for growth, redefining their paths and achieving sustained competitive advantage. Moreover, by shifting to offense, individuals and leaders can dictate the pace and direction of their industries, their influence, and the trajectory of their lives.

Transitioning from a reactive to a proactive stance is a significant shift that requires more than just a change in mindset; however, it demands dedication, practice, and the right tools. We understand that simply deciding to be proactive doesn't instantly transform your actions or approach. It takes consistent effort to integrate this perspective into daily operations and decision-making processes.

This is why we aren't just inviting you to adopt a new perspective; we are equipping you with a powerful framework to make this shift achievable. Through *The Power of the Pivot*, we provide you with practical tools and strategies designed to help you take aligned actions consistently. These tools will support you in identifying opportunities, anticipating changes, and making decisions that not only protect your business but also propel it forward.

By embracing this approach and utilizing our PIVOT framework, you can transition from merely surviving *reactively* to thriving *proactively*. This journey won't be without its challenges. But with persistence and the right guidance, you can redefine your trajectory and achieve sustained success.

## EVERYONE PIVOTS, SO PIVOT *WELL*

If there is one thing we know and have unequivocally seen in our nearly fifteen years of entrepreneurship, it is that everyone pivots. Whether they have used the word pivot to describe the action or not, the process a person or business goes through to realign their external environment or existence with what they desire or how they feel is, in fact, a pivot.

Pivoting is fundamentally about alignment, like visiting a chiropractor for a misaligned back. It's the same decision when you pivot your life or business—the friction you feel needs to be addressed and released. Sometimes, the friction is acute, arising suddenly from an unexpected opportunity or a life circumstance that alters how you live and work. It can even come from a global event like a pandemic. Other times, the friction is chronic, lingering in the background of the mind or body for quite some time. It's more of an annoyance than a true problem (until it becomes one!). Like those financial strains that should be addressed, but just not today. Or those operational inefficiencies that are kind of annoying but not enough to stop conducting business.

The pivot typically comes when the pain of enduring the current reality is too high and requires a change. While some people visit the chiropractor on an ongoing basis to remain in alignment, others are willing to go only when they wake up unable to turn their head. Does that mean they're walking around out of alignment each week that they don't go see the chiropractor?

When you're faced with the same question, only you know the answer. You're the only one who can feel that tension inside your body, your business, or your life. How long will you choose to wait to address it? How drastic will the response have to be once the decision is made? The outcomes hinge on how effectively you manage this tension.

Drawing from our experience in building a seven-figure staffing business by staying true to our purpose, making the Inc. 5000 list for three consecutive years while maintaining our integrity, and consulting hundreds of businesses and leaders—from owner-operators to corporations and nonprofits—we have crafted this framework to be both practical and impactful. Our journey has provided us with invaluable insights into what it takes to pivot successfully and achieve sustained growth.

In the pages that follow, you can expect a comprehensive guide that begins with a couple of foundational chapters. These initial chapters will set the stage by exploring what a pivot is not and explaining the reactive versus the proactive mindset. Following this, each chapter will dive deeply into one component of the PIVOT framework, providing you with tools, strategies, and real-world examples to help you Prepare, Inspect, Visualize, Organize, and Transform your business.

By the end of this book, you will not only understand the necessity of pivoting but also have a clear, actionable plan to transition from reactive survival to proactive thriving. Let's embark on this transformative journey together, turning your defense into offense and aligning with the success you envision.

Are you ready?

Turn the page.

# CHAPTER 1

# The Perception of the Pivot

Do you know the story of how Apple introduced the iPod? It's a great example of how a pivot takes place.

In the early 2000s, Apple was primarily known for its Macintosh computers, which had a dedicated but niche following. The company needed a breakthrough product to establish itself as a leader in the consumer electronics market. They wanted to expand their market share in the electronics market, and just selling computers wasn't going to cut it. This breakthrough came with the introduction of the iPod, a portable media player that revolutionized the way people listened to music. Apple was not the first to market with an MP3 player. In fact, they were actually a bit late to the game. MP3 players were already a household name and an object many already had in their pocket—which Apple benefitted from. But as soon as the iPod emerged on the scene, Apple essentially took over the market.

Released on October 23, 2001, the iPod was a game changer. With its sleek design, intuitive user interface, and ability to store a thousand songs in your pocket, the iPod soon became a cultural phenomenon. The market was already familiar with the function of an MP3 player, so to now have one that was aesthetically beautiful and offered greater storage than all other options, they immediately rose to the top of the market. By August 2004, Apple had 90.7 percent of the digital music player market.[2] The success of the iPod not only boosted Apple's revenue but also transformed the company's image into that of a cutting-edge innovator. Owning an iPod became a status symbol; any other MP3 player was simply subpar. Which was an important status to have for what comes next.

At this point in the story, are you seeing a pivot coming? Based on what you know or the information shared so far, can you think of any reason why Apple would want or need to pivot?

As the iPod dominated the market, Apple foresaw the convergence of digital devices and the increasing importance of mobile phones. Recognizing that the future lay in integrating multiple functionalities into a single device, Apple began developing a revolutionary new product—the iPhone. Unveiled by Steve Jobs on January 9, 2007, the iPhone combined a mobile phone, a widescreen iPod with touch controls, and an internet communications device in one. The first iPhone was released on June 29, 2007. The integration of music, telephony, and internet functionality

---

[2]Mike Musgrove, "IPod Helps Lift Apple's Fourth-Quarter Profit," *The Washington Post,* 2004, https://www.washingtonpost.com/archive/business/2004/10/14/ipod-helps-lift-apples-fourth-quarter-profit/271c7bb6-034a-4c85-8017-4b4eda5fa22b/.

marked a significant pivot for Apple. The sleek design, inno-vative integration of multiple functions, and the customer's familiarity with its functions as a result of using the iPod make this an immediate success.

But the iPhone's introduction led to a strategic shift that would ultimately cannibalize Apple's own iPod business. By incorporating an iPod into the iPhone, Apple rendered stand-alone MP3 players less necessary. Consumers now had a device that combined the functionality of an iPod with a phone and an internet browser in one compact unit.

Brilliant, right?

This pivot was deliberate and strategic. Apple understood that the market was moving toward multifunctional devices and that clinging to the stand-alone MP3 player market would eventually limit its growth. The company embraced this cannibalization, focusing on the broader potential of the smartphone market. They knew they would be stuck in a defensive position if they clung to just MP3 players. Instead, they positioned themselves offensively, putting that same technology into a more expensive and more multi-functional technology that fit in your pocket.

The decision to cannibalize the iPod with the iPhone paid off immensely. By 2008, the iPhone's sales had surpassed those of the iPod. Apple reported selling 6.1 million iPhones in the first five quarters after its release. This trend continued, and the iPhone became the cornerstone of Apple's product lineup and its primary revenue driver. As of 2020, Apple had sold over 1.5 billion iPhones, making it one of the most success-ful consumer electronics products in history. The iPod, once a revolutionary product, was officially discontinued in 2022. The iPhone's success also paved the way for the creation of an entire ecosystem of products and services, including the App Store, which launched in 2008 and became another significant revenue stream for the company.

## PIVOTS PRESENT OPPORTUNITIES

What can you learn from this?

Pivots are not just for failing businesses or products; when done well, they represent the ability to capitalize on opportunity. Apple's strategic pivot from the iPod to the iPhone is a textbook example of successful business adaptation and innovation. By anticipating market trends and embracing the cannibalization of its own products, Apple stayed ahead of the curve and redefined the technology landscape. The iPhone's introduction not only transformed Apple but also revolutionized the entire mobile phone industry, cementing Apple's position as a leader in global innovation. It wasn't just innovation either. The intentional choice to have design at the forefront also meant it stood out in a sector that historically has rather unattractive features. Even the decision to use white automatically meant it would become a status symbol. Though it was a risk to do this, it was staying true to the founder Steve Jobs' desires for everything to be beautiful (including the inside components of the phone), and so turned out to be an alignment aspect that paid off.

—➤ **Pivots are not just for failing businesses or products; when done well, they represent the ability to capitalize on opportunity.**

Doing that, however, was a major risk for Apple. It bet on itself in a way that a lot of business owners can't afford or perhaps wouldn't even be willing to do. The idea of canni-balizing one of your biggest sellers is probably beyond just scary and likely borders on stupid. But pivots don't have to be risky; although any business decision has inherent risk associated with it, strategic pivots can actually mitigate risk by allowing the business to gradually adapt to external pressures and evolving markets. By staying true to the passions and desires innate in you as the leader, you can differentiate yourself in the market. To this day, Apple has some of the most beautifully designed stores. They intentionally include sleek and aesthetic elements to curate the experience a customer feels when engaging with their products. You may think you are shopping in a high-fashion store, but you're actually interacting with pieces of technology. Let's look at another example that exemplifies how to mitigate risk with a pivot.

Founded in 1997 by Reed Hastings and Marc Randolph, Netflix initially offered a subscription-based DVD rental service that allowed customers to rent DVDs online and have them delivered by mail. This model was a significant improvement over traditional brick-and-mortar rental stores (like Blockbuster), offering greater convenience and a vast selection of titles. By 2005, Netflix had shipped its billionth DVD and had over 4.2 million subscribers. The DVD rental service was highly successful, but Hastings and his team foresaw the potential of digital distribution and the eventual decline of physical media.

Recognizing the growing influence of the internet and advancements in broadband technology, Netflix began experimenting with streaming video as early as 2007. On January 16, 2007, Netflix announced a new service called Watch Now, which allowed subscribers to stream movies and TV shows directly to their computers. This was revolutionary; no one was watching shows on their computers. Which is why Netflix was risk averse, not necessarily wanting to go all in on this offer right from the jump. So, this service was initially limited and offered a modest selection of content. But it marked the beginning of a significant strategic shift.

Netflix's transition from DVD rentals to streaming was gradual and carefully managed to mitigate risk. The company continued to invest in its DVD rental service while simultaneously building its streaming library and infrastructure. This dual approach allowed Netflix to maintain its existing customer base and revenue stream while exploring new opportunities in digital distribution. To ensure a smooth transition, Netflix negotiated licensing agreements with content providers to expand its streaming library. By 2010, the company had signed deals with major studios, like Warner Bros., Universal Pictures, and 20th Century Fox, significantly enhancing the variety and quality of its streaming offerings.

The shift to streaming was not without challenges. Netflix faced competition from established players, like Amazon and Hulu, as well as new entrants, like HBO Now (now Max) and Disney+. Additionally, the rapid growth of streaming required significant investments in technology and content acquisition. Netflix responded to these challenges by continuously innovating and expanding its service. In 2010, the company introduced streaming-only subscription plans, which allowed customers to access its streaming library without subscribing to the DVD rental service. This move further emphasized Netflix's commitment to streaming as its primary business model.

The company's focus on original content also played a crucial role in its success. In 2013, Netflix released its first original series, *House of Cards*, which received critical acclaim and demonstrated the potential of exclusive content to attract and retain subscribers. This strategy of producing high-quality original content helped Netflix differentiate itself from competitors and build a loyal subscriber base. They also were the first to release entire seasons of a show at once, creating virality around "binging" that we had not experienced prior. It ensured even more buzz for the shows they had created, as it created a cultural phenomenon that we hadn't been used to with weekly episodic drops of content from television. Netflix's pivot to streaming was a resounding success. By 2013, the company had more streaming subscribers than DVD rental customers, marking a significant milestone in its transformation. The DVD rental service, which had once been Netflix's core business, became increasingly marginalized as streaming took center stage.

Today, Netflix is the world's leading streaming service, with over 230 million subscribers worldwide as of 2023. The company's investment in original content has paid off, with hit series like *Stranger Things*, *The Crown*, and *The Witcher* attracting global audiences and driving subscriber growth. Netflix's strategic pivot from DVD rentals to streaming is a prime example of a company successfully navigating industry disruption and evolving consumer preferences. By gradually transitioning its business model and investing in digital distribution and original content, Netflix mitigated risk and positioned itself as a dominant player in the entertainment industry. This ability to adapt and innovate has cemented Netflix's status as a pioneer in the streaming era and a leader in the global media landscape.

It can feel intimidating to make a bold decision for business or life that isn't proven. In fact, we often suggest that clients start with a minimally viable option, put it into the market, and iterate on it endlessly until it proves itself. This is one of the most risk-averse ways of introducing something new, beta testing the idea, and getting customer buy-in at the same time—which is exactly what Netflix did. It's also a counterexample to Apple's decision.

## WHAT A PIVOT ISN'T

While you may be starting to get a concept of what a pivot *is*, it's equally important to understand what a pivot *isn't*. Being able to make the distinction will actually help you identify it better in yourself or your business.

**In order to actually pivot, you need a substantive internal change, which is aligned action.**

A pivot isn't a superficial change or minor adjustment in your strategy. It's not about tweaking a few details or making small, incremental improvements. A true pivot involves a fundamental shift in direction, often prompted by new insights or a reevaluation of your goals. Understanding this distinction is crucial to avoid mistaking minor course corrections for genuine pivots.

A pivot doesn't necessarily have to be a massive external change that everyone notices immediately, but it does require a fundamental shift. This means altering the underlying approach or strategy that guides your decisions and actions. For example, shifting your target market, changing your core product offering, and redefining your business model are all fundamental shifts. These changes go beyond surface-level adjustments and reflect a deep, internal realignment of your goals and methods.

In order to actually pivot, you need a substantive internal

change, which is aligned action. Let's look at a few examples that, on the surface, may seem like pivots but aren't actually.

## IS IT PR, OR IS IT A PIVOT?

In the wake of George Floyd's murder on May 25, 2020, a significant wave of protests and public outcry against racial injustice and police brutality swept across the United States and the world. In response to this societal reckoning, many companies hastily announced diversity, equity, and inclusion (DEI) initiatives, pledging to address systemic racism in their organizations. For some of these companies, however, the implementation of DEI measures was more about appearances and public relations than genuine internal transformation.

Following the widespread protests, numerous corporations released statements condemning racism and vowing to improve diversity and inclusion in their ranks. Social media was flooded with posts, hashtags, and commitments to change. Companies promised to hire more diverse talent, create inclusive work environments, and donate to racial justice organizations.

While the initial surge of DEI initiatives appeared promising, the subsequent actions of some companies revealed a lack of substantive change. In many cases, these measures were superficial and performative, designed to placate public sentiment rather than effect meaningful transformation. Some common characteristics of these performative DEI efforts included:

- **Token Appointments:** Appointing a chief diversity officer or creating a DEI committee without allocating

sufficient resources, authority, or a clear mandate to drive real change
- **One-Time Training Sessions:** Conducting one-off diversity training sessions that were more about checking a box than fostering an ongoing commitment to learning and improvement
- **Inadequate Follow-Through:** Announcing ambitious diversity goals without establishing concrete plans, timelines, or accountability mechanisms to achieve them
- **Marketing over Substance:** Prioritizing public relations campaigns and social media posts over genuine efforts to understand and address systemic issues in the organization

A true pivot involves a fundamental shift in strategy, operations, or culture. It requires an organization to realign its goals, processes, or values to adapt to new circumstances or insights. In contrast, performative DEI measures do not constitute a pivot because they fail to instigate real internal change. Key indicators that these efforts were more about PR than a genuine pivot include:

- **Persisting Inequities:** Despite public commitments, many companies saw little to no improvement in diversity metrics, such as representing minorities in leadership positions or closing pay gaps.
- **Retention and Morale Issues:** Employees from underrepresented groups continued to report feelings of exclusion, discrimination, and lack of support, leading to high turnover rates and low morale.
- **Short-Lived Initiatives:** Once the immediate public pressure subsided, many companies quietly scaled back or abandoned their DEI initiatives, demonstrating a lack of sustained commitment.

The distinction between a genuine pivot and a PR move is critical. A true pivot involves deep, lasting change that reshapes an organization's identity and operations. In contrast, the superficial DEI measures that some companies adopted in the aftermath of George Floyd's murder exemplify how public relations efforts can be mistaken for substantive change. These actions, driven more by the desire to manage public perception than to confront and dismantle systemic inequities, ultimately fail to transform an organization's internal culture and structure. For real progress, companies must move beyond performative gestures and commit to ongoing, meaningful action that addresses the root causes of inequality.

## NEXT STEPS V. A TRUE PIVOT

In the world of business strategy, the terms *pivot* and *next steps* are often used interchangeably, but they signify fundamentally different actions. While we are not interested in being the pivot police by chasing after every person who misuses the word, it is important to get into a bit of the semantics around whether something is a pivot or not. Understanding the distinction is crucial for recognizing when a company is making a significant change in direction versus simply progressing along its existing path.

Taking the next step is about following a planned trajectory toward a long-term goal. It involves incremental changes and improvements that align with the company's existing strategy and objectives. These steps are necessary to advance toward the desired outcome but do not constitute a fundamental shift in direction. As you will learn in our PIVOT framework—Prepare, Inspect, Vision, Organize, and Transform—the back half of the work can be done on an ongoing basis. It's a way to conduct business and not just pivot. First, you set your *vision* (which happens at the *V*). After that, organizing what comes next and transforming are steps you can repeat over and over to continue working toward the next phase in your goals.

Tesla, the electric vehicle (EV) manufacturer, provides a clear example of taking the necessary next steps rather than making a pivot. From its inception, Tesla's mission has been to accelerate the world's transition to sustainable energy. To achieve this, the company needed to address the challenge of battery production, which is critical for both electric vehicles and energy storage solutions.

- **Initial Focus:** Tesla started with high-performance electric cars, aiming to prove that EVs could be superior to gasoline vehicles.
- **Expansion into Energy:** To support its EVs and broaden its impact, Tesla began developing energy storage products, such as the Powerwall and Powerpack.
- **Gigafactories:** Recognizing the need for large-scale battery production, Tesla built gigafactories to produce batteries at a scale that would reduce costs and support its vehicles and energy products.

Each of these steps was a logical progression toward Tesla's overarching goal of moving the world to sustainable energy. The expansion into battery production and the construction of gigafactories were necessary steps to support its EVs and energy products, not a fundamental change in direction. Tesla remained focused on its mission, continually moving closer to its desired outcome. It's an example you should keep in mind when you get to the vision chapter. What you identify for yourself is intended to take you deep into the future of what you want. You'll use the Organize chapter to then set the action plan of goals, as Tesla did with its different phases of approaches.

A pivot involves a significant change in strategy, often in response to new insights, market conditions, or failures. It means altering the company's course to explore a new business model, target market, or product offering. A pivot is driven by the need to adapt to changing circumstances or find a more viable path to success.

## A REBRAND IS NOT A PIVOT

A rebrand and a pivot are two distinct strategies that businesses use to adapt to market conditions, update their image, or shift their strategic direction. However, they involve different levels of change in the organization. A rebrand typically involves changing a company's visual identity—its colors, fonts, logos, and imagery—and updating its messaging to better align with current market trends or customer perceptions. While a rebrand can refresh a company's image and make it more appealing, it does not necessarily involve fundamental changes in the company's target demographic, product offerings, or core business strategy.

Under a newly appointed creative director, Giovanna Battaglia Engelbert, Swarovski has undergone a significant rebranding effort. Engelbert, appointed as Swarovski's first-ever global creative director, introduced a new creative vision that includes:

- **New Collections:** Launching new jewelry lines, such as the Una family, symbolizing timeless love
- **Product Expansion:** Introducing new product categories, like eyewear and watches

- **Retail Innovation:** Reimagining retail spaces with flagship and Wonderlab stores[3] in key locations

Despite these substantial changes in visual identity and product expansion, Swarovski's core business remains focused on luxury jewelry and crystal products that target a similar demographic but with a fresh and contemporary aesthetic. These changes constitute a rebrand because they involve surface-level updates and expansion in the existing business model rather than a fundamental shift in the company's market focus or core offerings. It is worth mentioning, however, that these updated aesthetics and products did end up attracting a new audience. Therefore, they may seem to be a pivot toward a different target market.

For example, Swarovski ended up landing a collaboration with SKIMS,[4] which attracted an audience who likely otherwise would not have shopped at or purchased from the brand. Even SKIMS founder Kim Kardashian herself is quoted as saying, "I've always been a Swarovski girl.[5]" So, simply collaborating with her does not constitute a pivot, and increasing its market share as a result of a strategic collaboration also does not constitute a pivot.

On the other hand, sometimes a rebrand *can* launch a pivot. Instagram, the popular social media platform, provides a clear example of this.

---

[3]Angel Nemov, "Swarovski's New Chapter: Giovanna Engelbert on Her Colourful Vision for the Future of Jewellery," *Perfect Magazine*, 2021, https://www.theperfectmagazine.com/features/swarovskis-new-chapter-giovanna-engelbert-on-her-colourful-vision-for-the-future-of-jewellery.

[4]Iara Gonzalez, "Swarovski and Skims Came Together for a Bedazzled Collection," *Harper's Bazaar*, 2023, https://www.harpersbazaar.com/fashion/a45712930/swarovski-x-skims-collection-launch-kim-kardashian-interview/.

[5]Kevin LeBlanc, "Kim Kardashian Talks Crystals, Body Jewelry, and Her Swarovski x Skims Collaboration," *ELLE*, 2023, https://www.elle.com/fashion/celebrity-style/a45723868/kim-kardashian-swarovski-skims-collaboration-interview/.

- **Original Concept:** Instagram started as Burbn, a location-based check-in app that allowed users to check into places, earn points for hanging out with friends, and post pictures of their meetups (think like Yelp).
- **Pivot:** Observing that users were primarily using the photo-sharing feature, the founders, Kevin Systrom and Mike Krieger, decided to pivot the app's focus. They stripped away all other features and relaunched it as Instagram, concentrating solely on sharing photos with filters.
- **New Direction:** Instagram's new focus on simplicity and its unique photo-sharing capabilities resonated with users, leading to rapid growth and its eventual acquisition by Facebook for $1 billion in 2012.

This shift from Burbn to Instagram was a true pivot because it involved a fundamental change in the product's core functionality and target market, leading to a completely different user experience and business trajectory.

Understanding the difference between a rebrand and a pivot is essential for businesses navigating their strategic journey. A rebrand involves changes to the company's visual identity and messaging without altering its core offerings or market strategy. Swarovski's creative overhaul under Giovanna Battaglia Engelbert is a prime example, where visual and product updates were made while the fundamental business focus remained the same. In contrast, a pivot entails a fundamental shift in the company's business model, product, or market focus. Instagram's transformation from Burbn to a photo-sharing platform exemplifies a pivot, demonstrating a deep change in direction that redefined the company's identity and growth path.

To recap: A pivot is not a PR move in an effort to save face.

It is not next steps in a larger existing plan. And it is not a rebrand (though a rebrand can occur as a result of a pivot).

Now that you understand what a pivot is not, we're shifting focus to what a pivot is. In the coming chapter, we'll start by defining a pivot. Next, we'll present pivoting from defensive and offensive postures. From there, we'll focus on how to transition from the former to the latter, then conclude with what results when this shift is made successfully.

If you agree that it is important to know what something is *not* but even more important to know what something actually is, let's jump in!

# CHAPTER 2
# The Purpose of the Pivot

As the old adage goes, the only constant is change. Despite knowing this, most people still resist it in earnest. This book isn't about convincing you that change is good or necessary; rather, it aims to offer a fresh perspective on change. Because no matter how hard you try, you will never avoid the inevitable in life, and change is one of those inevitabilities.

Regardless of how or why anyone enters the business world, once here, everyone recognizes that they are often at the mercy of situations and circumstances beyond their control. As is also true in life. Businesses, regardless of size or sector, encounter continuous flux that demands not just passive observation but active participation. The span ranges from seemingly trivial issues, like Instagram being down for the day, to foundation-shaking events, such as legislation altering the short-term rental market.

Many people start businesses with singular ideas about what those businesses will enable for them. They rarely look far enough down the road to truly anticipate anything that could disrupt their business models. To be fair, it's not entirely necessary to foresee every challenge. However, there is a key strategic perspective to be aware of, and that is what inspired this book. You have to recognize how much is and can be out of your control at any point in business or life. That's why the focus of any leader must evolve from merely reacting to unforeseen forces to proactively anticipating and shaping future dynamics.

As previously mentioned, the tool we recommend for achieving this proactive mindset is the pivot. By mastering the art of the pivot, you can turn disruptions into opportunities, ensuring your business not only survives but thrives in an ever-changing environment.

## WHAT IS A PIVOT?

So, what exactly is a pivot? A pivot in business typically refers to a fundamental shift in strategy or approach that an organization undertakes to adapt to changes in the market, capitalize on emerging opportunities, or mitigate risks. While many assume a pivot involves a massive change or abrupt right turn in a business, it often means rethinking key aspects of a business model, services offered, target market, or operational methods. This doesn't necessarily imply a major change; it can involve small, incremental adjustments. The goal is to realign how you do business to better suit current or future market dynamics.

A key word here: *alignment.* That's what this is all about—getting you, the human running the business or living your life, back into alignment with what you say, think, or know you want. You may have never done this work before, and that's okay. You're here now. Most people find themselves desiring or needing a pivot because of the friction they feel in their business or life. They're no longer happy—sometimes even miserable. They've experienced a life event that changed how they can approach their services, or there's a great opportunity that requires a business model update to align with it.

**A key word here: *alignment.* That's what this is all about— getting you, the human running the business or living your life, back into alignment with what you say, think, or know you want.**

There it is again—*alignment.* You're going to see it a lot because we hope you will perpetually feel in alignment with each business decision, the overall direction for your business, and the way you conduct yourself each day.

In many cases, you do not have the luxury of deciding when to pivot. Often, you are thrust into it by necessity. It might be due to life circumstances, like getting pregnant, needing to care for an ailing family member, or experiencing a sudden health change. Or it could be due to market conditions, regulatory changes, or a worldwide pandemic. Sometimes, a pivot is strategically done to take full advantage of an opportunity in front of you. Each business and person has different indicators that may signal the need for a pivot.

Significant changes in the market, such as new regulations,

shifting consumer preferences, the emergence of new technologies, or increased competitive pressure, often necessitate a reassessment of current strategies. This was evident with the rise and plateau of the short-term rental market. Many owners entered the market, rapidly shifting demand. Then, waves of regulation drastically reduced and restricted the market. This left many investors in dire situations in which they had to pivot or leave the business altogether.

Similarly, if your business consistently underperforms on critical metrics compared to industry benchmarks, this could indicate that your existing approach is no longer effective. We saw a lot of this in the online space after the onset of COVID-19. So many coaches popped up online, and many people, being at home, were buying courses and spending generously. Then, in 2022, most of the selling tactics stopped working effectively, buyers became more skeptical, and there was a shift away from online coaches. As a result, many people had to leave the industry while others massively shifted their marketing and sales strategies.

Opportunities can also prompt a pivot. The emergence of new market segments, technological advances, or other opportunities that align with your company's strengths but require a different business approach can justify a strategic shift. We're seeing a lot of this with AI. Brand-new businesses are popping up, and extensions of known businesses are creating new offerings to keep up with changing technology. In the staffing industry, we are seeing AI used for everything from recruitment to sifting resumes and conducting initial interviews. In the interior design space that Maurice works in, AI is now creating entire faux interiors. You can hardly tell if you're looking at a real or AI-generated interior design. Almost everyone, from individual creators to Fortune 500 companies, is looking at how to incorporate AI into workflows. It's an opportunity that no business owner, content creator, or industry leader can afford to miss.

Internally, challenges like declining employee morale, high turnover rates, or operational inefficiencies might also necessitate a pivot, especially if these issues threaten the business's long-term health. We saw a lot of this on the heels of COVID-19. Employee morale declined due to increased stress and isolation from remote work, leading to lower engagement and loyalty. Driven by pandemic-induced burnout and the desire for more flexible work conditions, high turnover rates surged, with many employees seeking better compensation, benefits, and work-life balance. Additionally, operational inefficiencies arose from the rapid transition to remote work and frequent hiring due to high turnover, disrupting business continuity[6] and productivity.[7] Corporations across America were forced to come up with alternative work environments and recruitment strategies to retain or recruit workers. In an economy where there were twice as many job openings as available workers, corporations had to pivot toward accepting and acknowledging their employees' demands.

These aren't the only reasons a company or individual may need to pivot. There are far more nuanced versions of each of these and several more. The point here is to demonstrate that sometimes, business owners are presented with opportunities, and other times, they are thrust into decisions. It can be gradual, or it can be a full fire drill, as was the case with the pandemic.

---

[6]Larry Akinyooye and Eric Nezamis, "As the COVID-19 Pandemic Affects the Nation, Hires and Turnover Reach Record Highs in 2020," *Monthly Labor Review*, U.S. Bureau of Labor Statistics, 2021, https://www.bls.gov/opub/mlr/2021/article/as-the-covid-19-pandemic-affects-the-nation-hires-and-turnover-reach-record-highs-in-2020.htm.

[7]Jill Chapman, "Post-pandemic Employee Turnover: Why It's Happening and What to Do About It," *Insperity*, 2021, https://www.insperity.com/blog/post-pandemic-employee-turnover-why-its-happening-and-what-to-do-about-it/.

While a business can have contingency plans and operational backups for "just in case" moments, unforeseen events will always arise. Just ask Farmers Insurance. Its "Seen It. Covered It." commercials showcase unbelievable claims that allow it to proclaim, "We know a thing or two because we've seen a thing or two." The range of potential mishaps and misfortunes is vast, including legal issues, sudden death, loss of a key management-level employee, and natural disasters.

As previously mentioned, the tool we recommend for navigating these unpredictable waters is the pivot. By mastering the art of the pivot, you can turn disruptions into opportunities, ensuring your business not only survives but thrives in an ever-changing environment.

## DEFENSE

To some extent, no matter how much planning, strategy, or foresight you've put into preparing for and avoiding disaster, it will eventually find a way to your doorstep. When you're in this situation, you're on defense.

Defensive pivots are primarily reactive. Much like a sports team that adjusts its strategy in real time to block advances from opponents, a defensive pivot in business is aimed at mitigating immediate dangers that threaten operational stability. They are implemented in response to urgent challenges that pose immediate risks to a business's stability or profitability.

Consider a restaurant in Chicago called Frontier. When the pandemic forced the closure of dining spaces, Frontier introduced a takeout menu and meal kits for families to cook at home. This pivot quickly became a significant revenue source, comprising about 70 percent of Frontier's weekly sales. The restaurant also started offering live virtual cooking classes to complement the meal kits, enabling it to maintain business and engage with customers during the pandemic.[8] This shift allowed the restaurant to continue operations and maintain revenue streams even when its primary business model was threatened.

Or think about The Cookie Cups, a brick-and-mortar bakery in Minnesota. Faced with fewer in-person customers and the need to adapt, owner Nicole Pomije transitioned her bakery to focus on delivery through platforms like Grubhub and DoorDash. To further innovate, she introduced cooking kits that could be shipped nationwide, allowing customers to recreate The Cookie Cups experience at home. This shift not only helped sustain the business during tough times but also expanded its market reach significantly beyond local customers[9].

**A defensive pivot in business is aimed at mitigating immediate dangers that threaten operational stability.**

The primary outcome of a defensive pivot is often the stabilization of operations and preservation of cash flow, akin to a sports team managing to hold off the opposition and prevent a score. The sports adage "Bend, don't break" refers to allowing the opposing team to get very close to scoring and perhaps even scoring fewer points (a field goal in football, which is worth three points, instead of a touchdown, which is worth six). Playing defense is about holding the line and mitigating as

---

[8]Sean Peek, "5 Restaurant Industry Pandemic Pivots," *US Chamber of Commerce,* 2020, https://www.uschamber.com/co/good-company/growth-studio/restaurant-industry-pandemic-pivots.

[9]Sean Peek, "5 Restaurant Industry Pandemic Pivots," *US Chamber of Commerce,* 2020, https://www.uschamber.com/co/good-company/growth-studio/restaurant-industry-pandemic-pivots.

much repercussion as possible. While necessary and potentially effective in the short term, however, defensive pivots do have their limitations.

Frequent defensive shifts without a clear, overarching strategy can lead to brand confusion and strategic drift, which is when a company's plans slowly stop matching what is happening in the world around it. Like a coach constantly switching strategies, you're just reacting to what the opposition is doing. You're not actually playing your game. You're playing someone else's. That means the other team is in control. This can disorient and fatigue your players and supporters alike, eroding trust and cohesion. No one wants to play a game or root for a team that the opponent is manipulating. Being out-coached, out-strategized, and outplayed is no fun.

Always being on the defensive prevents you from addressing the strategic weaknesses that require such pivots in the first place. When a company consistently reacts to external pressures without proactive planning, it fails to identify and resolve the core issues that necessitate these defensive measures. This reactive approach can lead to a cycle of short-term fixes, diverting attention from long-term strategy and innovation. Without addressing the underlying weaknesses, the business risks stagnating and losing its competitive edge. By focusing only on immediate threats, companies miss opportunities to strengthen their foundational strategy and anticipate future challenges proactively. This imbalance can ultimately undermine a company's sustainability and growth potential.

So, while defensive pivots are crucial for short-term survival and crisis management, they need to be carefully balanced with the company's long-term strategic goals. Many businesses unknowingly remain in this defensive stance, focusing on justifying and defending their market position. Often, years into their journey, they realize they've been reacting to others instead of leading with their own strategy.

## OFFENSE

The other side of the game is offense. While defensive actions safeguard the present, offensive strategies propel a business forward. These steps help companies get ahead, not just protect and maintain what they have. This transition marks a shift from survival mode to a growth-oriented approach, leveraging both current stability and emerging market opportunities to aggressively expand and innovate. By leveraging the stability achieved through defensive measures, companies can now focus on harnessing and capitalizing on emerging market opportunities with an aggressive, forward-thinking mindset. This change is not merely strategic but also psychological, as it reorients the entire business toward expansion and innovation rather than mere endurance.

> **Offensive strategies propel a business forward.**

An offensive pivot involves proactive strategizing to exploit opportunities and drive growth. This growth is not just for its own sake. It actually moves you closer to the vision you have for yourself and your business. Unlike the reactive nature of defensive pivots, offensive pivots are planned and executed with the aim of transforming the business in a way that not only responds to but also anticipates market demands. This is about taking control of the game, scheming and strategizing on how to score, and utilizing your team's skills and talents to outperform and outplay the opponent. You're now playing your game.

The transition to an offensive strategy is not just about growing bigger—it's about growing smarter and becoming more influential in the industry. It's a comprehensive shift that impacts every aspect of the organization, including your personal development and emotions related to the business. It involves reimagining the daily operations, redefining your vision for both life and business, and reorganizing and strategizing priorities. Ultimately, it transforms your entire approach to doing business.

At the core of this shift is personal development. Business owners must evolve, expanding their skills and emotional resilience to navigate this new approach effectively. As they pivot to offensive strategies, they will often experience a wide range of emotions—from the excitement of pursuing new opportunities to the anxiety of stepping into uncharted territories. Managing these emotions and channeling them into productive, strategic actions is crucial. In many cases, this work will actually be harder than the tactical aspects of what will change in your business.

The transition also fundamentally changes how day-to-day operations are managed. When your entire perspective changes from simply defending and maintaining what you have to pursuing and creating what you want, the way you move in business will look different. From decision-making processes to resource allocation, every operational aspect must align with the vision you have for your business. These operational shifts ensure that it not only keeps pace with industry developments but also anticipates future trends.

A growth-oriented strategy necessitates that you reevaluate both your personal vision and your long-term goals for your business. This vision expands to encompass financial targets and truly capture the essence and core values of how you want to show up in the world. Your business is an extension of you—a how in the mission of your why. And it will be the vehicle you use to do your life's work. It requires a holistic view of where you want the business to go and what kind of legacy you intend to create, reflecting deeper aspirations that resonate with your values and life goals.

With a new vision comes the need to reorganize and strategize priorities in the business. This process involves setting clear, strategic priorities that align with the long-term vision and ensuring that every decision is focused on achieving these objectives. It requires a meticulous approach to planning and execution, in which short-term actions are steps toward fulfilling the broader goals. Inevitably, there will be times when you find yourself back on defense. In these moments, it is important that you recognize them as a rest break, not a complete detour on the way to your destination. This strategic realignment helps maintain focus and ensures that your efforts are concentrated on the stated vision.

Ultimately, embracing an offensive, growth-oriented strategy transforms the company's total existence and way of doing business. This new approach becomes ingrained in the company's culture, influencing how decisions are made, how risks are approached, and how opportunities are seized. It fosters a culture of innovation, resilience, and proactive engagement with what comes next. This not only helps navigate the complexities of the business world but also allows you to actively shape your own future. You're playing your own game, not being manipulated into playing someone else's.

These transitions are ultimately what make up our PIVOT framework.

- **Prepare:** Develop the necessary personal self-awareness and emotional fortitude to endure this transition.

- **Investigate:** Become curious about what's working and what's not in your business and begin identifying what changes need to be made.
- **Vision:** Before you begin reorganizing and reprioritizing all aspects of your business, first create the visual of what you truly want for yourself.
- **Organize:** Develop the road map and prioritize next steps to strategically align your business's everyday actions with playing on offense and pursuing your vision.
- **Transform:** Acknowledge all the ways you are a completely different business owner and are operating a business you had only ever dreamed of. Keep playing your own game.

## MAKING THE SHIFT

How will you know when you are ready to make the shift? We can tell you with certainty that if your business is not currently aligned with your why or purpose, it is time to make the shift. If you've not considered whether it is aligned, then the time is now to start. What is the point of providing your product or service if it is not anchored in your why or purpose? If you thought the point was some version of "To make money," we'd encourage you to consider what making money will do for you when you encounter a major setback, unexpected change in the market, or significant business challenge. There are millions of different ways to make money. Doing it in a way that provides deeper fulfillment will help you persevere.

Money alone is not a sustainable motivator during tough times. Instead, a clear purpose provides direction, resilience, and a deeper sense of fulfillment. When your business is aligned with your core values and purpose, it becomes easier to navigate obstacles and adapt to change. Your purpose acts as a guiding star, ensuring that every decision and pivot moves you closer to your ultimate vision. Of course, every choice you make comes with some level of risk—a topic many business owners falsely believe is mitigated when playing defense.

> **➤ When your business is aligned with your core values and purpose, it becomes easier to navigate obstacles and adapt to change.**

The shift from a defensive to an offensive strategic stance in business is characterized by several key features that collectively signify a business's readiness and commitment to proactively shape its future. While it's likely that you've been playing a mix of both offense and defense, it's very easy to get stuck in a defensive mindset. The longer you stay there, the harder it becomes to pivot back to offense. Making the shift to an offensive strategy, however, involves a marked change in how a company views challenges and opportunities while signaling a profound evolution in its strategic operations and mindset.

One of the primary characteristics of this shift is the movement from a reactive posture, where actions are primarily responses to external pressures or circumstances, to a proactive approach that seeks to anticipate and influence. This involves not just adapting to changes but setting the agenda, driving innovation, and being a market leader rather than a follower. This brings us to risk, a topic that many business owners think is safer when playing defense but is actually just an illusion.

In a defensive mode, risk management focuses on minimizing and avoiding risks. During an offensive shift, however, the approach to risk transforms into risk engagement, where risks are viewed as opportunities for growth. Shifting from seeing what comes your way as opportunities instead of obstacles completely changes how you can leverage your resources and take advantage of situations that can significantly alter the trajectory of your life and business.

With that comes strategic expansion and growth. For example, we consulted with several business owners who had brick-and-mortar locations, and they were able to expand into larger physical spaces previously perceived as unavailable to them. At one point, we consulted with four different business owners through the construction and development of spaces that at least doubled their size. These opportunities were not visible when the owners had a defensive mindset; however, these spaces became clear options once they solved most of their problems and strategically positioned themselves for expansion. These were not random but driven by strategic goals and a clear vision for their company's future.

It's unrealistic to think that expanding into double the amount of physical space is possible while you're putting out (literal or figurative) fires in the foundational aspects of your business. These shifts and opportunities often come after the defensive strategy has been stabilized. This is why it's imperative to investigate and determine what needs to be shored up before going into offense mode. While it can be fun and exciting to discuss all that is possible while playing offense, the defensive component cannot be overlooked or dismissed. We've included tools, such as the SWOT analysis and the included vision activity, to support your pivot whenever you need it.

# LEADERSHIP AND CULTURE

A successful pivot toward an offensive approach is not only marked by strategic and operational shifts. It also requires strong leadership and a supportive company culture. Neither of these characteristics is inherent, yet both must be developed and nurtured to effectively conduct and maintain the pivot. While we won't dive deeply into leadership in this section, it is important not to overlook its necessity. The role of leadership in this context extends beyond traditional management functions; it involves visionary thinking, an aptitude for risk, anticipating future trends, and the ability to instill a culture that not only tolerates but embraces change and innovation. Leadership is not limited to others; it is about self as well. Your ability to create and develop all of these aspects in yourself and your business, regardless of whether you manage or oversee other workers, is crucial.

During this transition, it is important to recognize that you will be developing as a leader. You will question yourself and whether you've chosen the right path forward. At times, you may even question your worthiness and abilities, wondering if you have the capabilities to take this on. These internal conversations are normal, and the turbulence you may feel in yourself or the business is something to be heard and acknowledged. You must become adept at understanding yourself, your business, and the market overall to truly determine the appropriate or necessary timing for these changes.

As the leader of the business and your life, you are called upon to make decisions that may feel overwhelming or have larger implications than you are comfortable with. It often feels safer (and easier) to remain on defense because the task there is straightforward: hold the line. In contrast, a world of endless possibility exists when on offense, but pursuing this uncertainty is often much scarier than staying within the confines of what is known. This fear of the unknown can make the pursuit of your desires intimidating, leading your mind to keep you small and safe. To overcome this, you must develop trust not only in your own resilience and ability to bounce back from setbacks but also in your team's resilience and capabilities.

**This dual capability— shifting gears between strategies as situations evolve— demands a deep belief in yourself and your ability to adapt, as well as a commitment to continuous learning.** Leaders who adeptly manage the interplay between offense and defense in business strategy possess a nuanced understanding of the business landscape. You can make proactive decisions that drive growth (offensive) while ensuring safeguards are in place to protect your business during downturns or unexpected events (defensive). Both approaches can coexist effectively. This dual capability—shifting gears between strategies as situations evolve—demands a deep belief in yourself and your ability to adapt, as well as a commitment to continuous learning. When you navigate this balance effectively, it instills a culture of agility and prudence in your organization and your life. You train yourself to value growth opportunities and maintain risk awareness, thinking strategically by always seeking growth prospects while being mindful of potential risks.

The finesse required to balance offensive and defensive pivots defines the caliber of leadership and sets the cultural tone for the organization. It's a dynamic interplay that demands vigilance, adaptability, and strategic foresight, ultimately creating an approach that prepares you not only to survive but to thrive, regardless of the challenges you face.

# FROM PROBLEM TO POSSIBILITY

Once you've established the importance of balancing offensive and defensive strategies, it's crucial to understand how this balance transforms your approach to business and life's challenges. When you reframe your understanding of what a pivot means for your business, you fundamentally transform your approach to both challenges and opportunities. Shifting your perspective from viewing pivots as merely reactionary measures to seeing them as proactive strategies enables you to transition your mindset from one that dwells on problems to one that sees potential. Instead of perceiving changes and challenges as obstacles, you begin to view them as opportunities for growth and innovation. You might wonder, *Why is this being presented to me? How can I take advantage of this? What is the opportunity here?* This change in perception is transformative, altering not just strategic decisions but your entire approach to business ownership, and even life.

Traditionally, pivots might be seen as last-ditch efforts to save a faltering business or respond to an unexpected market downturn, or grapple with an unexpected life circumstance. By shifting your perspective, however, you can start to recognize pivots as opportunities to rethink and possibly enhance your business model, explore new opportunities, or innovate products and services in ways that align more closely with your goals, what your customers want, or emerging market opportunities. This proactive approach encourages you to continually ask how you can improve, what new value you can create, and how you can differentiate yourself in the marketplace. This focus on possibility brings excitement and energy to the process.

Transitioning from a problem-focused to a possibility-focused mindset can do more than merely change your attitude toward difficulties; it transforms your entire approach to decision-making, problem-solving, and strategic thinking. A problem-focused mindset views challenges as hurdles or obstacles that need to be overcome. This perspective often leads to a defensive stance, where the primary goal is mitigation, containment, or avoidance. While effective for immediate crisis management, this approach can limit creative thinking and reduce opportunities to a series of issues to be solved. It can instill a sense of constraint and urgency that prioritizes short-term solutions over long-term sustainability and innovation.

**Shifting your perspective from viewing pivots as merely reactionary measures to seeing them as proactive strategies enables you to transition your mindset from one that dwells on problems to one that sees potential.**

In contrast, a possibility-focused mindset reframes these same challenges as opportunities for growth, learning, and innovation. This paradigm encourages looking beyond the immediate inconvenience or threat of a situation to explore what new outcomes could be achieved by addressing the underlying challenge. With this mindset, every challenge you face becomes a potential springboard for growth. Economic pressures, competitive threats, and changes in consumer behavior are no longer just problems to be mitigated. They are opportunities to strengthen the business, perhaps by streamlining operations, identifying cost efficiencies, or creating products and services that better meet the needs of a changing demographic.

Once this mindset shift is embraced, it becomes a perpetual mode of operation. You start to view all aspects of your business or life through the lens of possibility and opportunity. This continuous search for improvement and responsiveness to change fosters an environment of sustained innovation and agility that can significantly enhance your longevity as a business owner and, thereby, the business as its own entity.

Ultimately, this shift in perspective should be integrated into the company's long-term strategic planning. Companies that continuously align their strategies with the notion of pivots as opportunities ensure that they are always ready to capitalize on new developments rather than being sidelined by them. When you shift your perspective on what a pivot is and what it means for your business, you not only change how you approach current challenges but also how you plan for and imagine the future. This transition from a mindset focused on problems to one that sees possibilities and opportunities can fundamentally change the trajectory of a business, transforming its very fabric. It turns every challenge into a potential success story and every hurdle into a step toward innovation, driving the business forward with renewed vigor and vision. This paradigm shift not only makes handling challenges more engaging but also turns the entire organizational approach into one that is constantly learning, growing, and evolving.

➤ **This transition from a mindset focused on problems to one that sees possibilities and opportunities can fundamentally change the trajectory of a business, transforming its very fabric.**

We believe that every business, at some point, needs a pivot of some kind. In fact, we argue that conducting business is fundamentally an ongoing series of pivots. We view pivoting not just as a necessity but as the solution itself in the entrepreneurial journey. As opportunities and circumstances present themselves, it is critical that leaders consider where they are now and where a decision might take them, evaluating those existing and potential outcomes against their purpose or why.

That is how you begin to practice taking aligned action. The pivot is a vital tool that can be leveraged to do just that. We believe so strongly in it that it is the foundation of the framework you will learn in the following chapters.

Are you ready to PIVOT toward possibility?

# CHAPTER 3

# The Power of Preparation

The personal growth required for a business leader to effectively transition from a defensive to an offensive strategy involves deep internal work and often represents a more profound challenge than the tactical or strategic aspects of running a business. This process demands self-awareness, continuous learning, and the willingness to confront and change fundamental behaviors and beliefs.

Before you restructure your business for offense, you need to prepare yourself internally. External changes are straightforward and can be handled by almost anyone—they're the easy part. But this transition requires more than tactical adjustments; it demands a complete mindset overhaul. Simply adapting to protect yourself or your business won't propel you forward. You need to embrace optimism and reject pessimism. Developing a forward-thinking approach might feel vulnerable, but it's crucial for setting yourself up for greater success. This is not just a business change; it's a fundamental shift in how you approach life.

Choosing to make this transition is exactly that—a choice. While we are going to ask you to make that decision right now and demonstrate how to do it, know it's a choice that has to be made repeatedly in business and life. Even when you think you have mastered it in one area, it will show up somewhere else, continually challenging you to overcome this same hurdle. This is because this is a skill that needs to be developed over time. You do not simply arrive at mastery.

**Before you restructure your business for offense, you need to prepare yourself internally.**

Adopting a proactive mindset in business decisions, professional development, and life is often met with resistance, as society frequently endorses a reactive approach. This is because it's easier to blame other people and external circumstances for our shortcomings than to take accountability for falling short or making mistakes, even if it is our fault.

It is often perceived to be safer to stay on defense. When you're defending, your only responsibility is to protect your goal; you don't bear the burden of strategizing, vision casting, or considering hypotheticals. Your primary aim is simply to avoid failure. By just surviving, you can claim victory, pointing to any margin of success as proof of your accomplishments.

If you're content staying there, in your comfort zone, you might want to stop reading now. The remainder of this book will likely frustrate you, causing you to question why you ever considered leaving the safety of good enough in pursuit of great. There's plenty of room for those who are satisfied with good enough; they will live a life that is fine. You'll make just enough to get by and react to most challenges as they arise, which will lead to added stress and frustration. But you'll manage.

The rest of this book is for those who refuse to live like that. They are eager to position themselves for growth and seize every opportunity. The realm of possibility excites them, even if it's a bit terrifying, and they feel called to rise to the occasion. They want to call the shots, determine their pace, and choose their direction. They aspire to drive the evolution of their industry. Even if it's something they've only dreamed of, they feel called toward that dream and are committed to doing the work to achieve it.

If that's you, let's dive in.

## BUILDING THE FOUNDATION

Before we discuss the soft skills necessary for executing this work in your business, let's first acknowledge a few fundamental beliefs and behaviors. Specifically, you need to examine your ability to conduct internal reflection while maintaining self-awareness, discuss your level of emotional intelligence, and challenge some core beliefs you may hold.

Internal reflection is the exercise of pausing to critically examine your own underlying motivations, your decision-making patterns, and the effectiveness of your approach. The fact that you have picked up this book and read up to this chapter demonstrates a certain level of self-reflection. It involves deliberately taking time to contemplate your thoughts, decisions, behaviors, and leadership style. This introspective practice is crucial as it helps you gain deeper insights into your strengths and weaknesses, understand your impact on others, and assess how your actions align with your strategic goals. This culminates in a level of self-awareness necessary to shift from reactive to proactive behavior.

There will be times when your ego is challenged or you find that you have to slow down instead of speeding up. Through self-awareness, achieved via internal reflection, you can manage these situations effectively. This knowledge allows you to understand your own biases, fears, and limitations, providing the opportunity to set aside emotions during decision-making. This enables you to be as objective and unbiased as possible, then act in the best interest of the business.

This brings us to emotional intelligence (EI), which refers to your capability to recognize, understand, manage, and utilize emotions effectively in yourself and others. For business owners and leaders, particularly those managing strategic pivots, high emotional intelligence is crucial. It influences how you lead during times of change, manage stress, and communicate with your teams, including the internal conversations you have with yourself and the messaging you put forward.

Emotional intelligence is essential for leaders navigating a pivot, especially when bringing team members or clients along. How you manage yourself, your stress, your emotions, and others' emotions is crucial. Your ability to manage emotions, empathize with employees and clients, and navigate the interpersonal dynamics of change management will significantly impact your success.

Developing emotional intelligence equips you to handle the interpersonal and organizational challenges of a business pivot. It helps you foster a more collaborative, resilient workplace culture and lead change effectively. This involves regular internal reflection, feedback, active listening, empathy exercises, and the practical application of emotional intelligence principles in daily interactions and decision-making.

Finally, you need to address challenging core beliefs. Personal growth during this pivot requires questioning and sometimes overturning long-held beliefs about business, leadership, and success. This might include rethinking how you were taught to do business, examining your beliefs about the difficulty of business and the ease of making money, or redefining what success and leadership mean to you.

**➤ This process involves critically examining and reassessing the fundamental assumptions and principles guiding your decision-making, behaviors, and interactions in the business environment.**

This process involves critically examining and reassessing the fundamental assumptions and principles guiding your decision-making, behaviors, and interactions in the business environment. Your views on risk, failure, control, or collaboration might hold you back from making this pivot. Many business owners struggle with perceptions of control and risk, which are characteristics we will address next as we discuss what needs to be shed to grow into the business owner you aspire to be.

These beliefs can be deeply ingrained and challenging to alter. This work takes practice and often requires courage, humility, and a commitment to personal growth. It involves not just changing one's mind but often changing the direction of your entire organization. Give yourself grace. This work is done over several years and thousands of hours of practice, not just in a single sitting or by reading a book.

A leader's personality plays a pivotal role in successfully shifting from a defensive to an offensive strategy in business. This transformation requires not just strategic acumen but also significant personal growth and adaptation. Here are some key characteristics you'll need to cultivate and some you might need to shed, along with the emotional challenges you must confront during this shift.

## CHARACTERISTICS TO SHED

These characteristics may have served you up to this point, but they keep you playing small. They force you to stay safe and at your comfort level while also convincing you that they're necessary and serve the greater ends you're attempting to achieve. Risk aversion, pessimism, micromanagement, an excessive need for control, and a short-term focus, while potentially useful in stabilizing operations during turbulent times, can significantly impede a company's ability to adopt more aggressive and forward-looking strategies. We can assure you that they have no place in where you are going. So, we invite you to review them and then ceremonially release them.

### RISK AVERSION

While cautious analysis is important, excessive risk aversion can stifle growth and innovation. You need to become comfortable with the calculated risks that accompany offensive strategies. This is why we develop thorough strategies, including contingency plans, and talk through the what-ifs that may come up. It's not about dismissing risk altogether but making informed and educated decisions with a cost-benefit analysis to determine the best steps forward.

**In Practice:** Start with a small pilot or beta sample idea to test this out for yourself. Choose something with limited exposure (or risk) and take an action that you otherwise wouldn't take because of potential risk. Taking small actions over time will build your confidence in taking larger risks or more risks on an ongoing basis. This is a muscle that you have to flex by repeatedly proving to yourself that taking risks can result in a positive outcome. We're retraining your brain to associate risk with reward instead of failure.

## PESSIMISM

Leaders who are used to bracing for the worst (a common defensive posture) may find it difficult to adopt the optimistic outlook that an offensive strategy requires. Many of us have been taught that being pessimistic, or even skeptical, is a protective measure in a world where seemingly nothing can be trusted. Pessimism is a negative emotion that fosters resentment and cynicism, dampening enthusiasm and creativity. When you consistently expect the worst, you are less likely to pursue innovative ideas or invest in new opportunities due to fear of failure.

**In Practice:** Instead of always waiting for the other shoe to drop, practice positive reinforcement by celebrating small wins and progress, not just final outcomes. Reflect on successes, however minor, to shift focus from what could go wrong to what has gone right. In time, you will build a more positive outlook toward opportunities, which also helps shed the risk-averse characteristic. Shedding pessimism in favor of a balanced, optimistic view can help inspire confidence and drive in an organization.

## MICROMANAGEMENT

As businesses pivot, leaders must trust their teams and delegate effectively. Often, the exact opposite happens. Leaders dive deeper into all nuances and details, inserting themselves into every decision that needs to be made, thereby creating a bottleneck in their businesses. In our experience, micromanagement (and control, which comes next) is rooted in a lack of trust and proper processes. This reduces the autonomy of your workers and team members (including clients) and slows down processes and efficiency.

**In Practice:** Take inventory of all tasks that you personally do not need to be associated with. Identify someone else who can make those decisions instead, even if they need structure or feedback on how to do it effectively. Allow leeway for their how to look different than yours, focusing only on the outcome of the task being completed. Use regular check-ins rather than constant oversight to give feedback and guidance, empowering team members and building mutual trust. Letting go of micromanagement allows for more agility and faster decision-making at all levels.

> **Micromanagement is rooted in a lack of trust and proper processes.**

## CONTROL

While related to micromanagement, the need for control extends to a broader tendency to oversee all aspects of the operation personally. Sometimes, this is done out of necessity, as most business owners are the only ones working (or they at least started out that way), and releasing the details and oversight of specific areas is scary and hard. But, when leaders exert too much control, it can lead to dependency, where employees feel unable to act without explicit instructions. This undermines their ability to handle responsibilities independently and can stifle leadership development in the team. Overcontrol can also make an organization rigid, inflexible, and unable to adapt quickly to new challenges or take advantage of spontaneous opportunities that arise.

**In Practice:** Similar to the exercise for micromanagement, focus on developing and communicating clear, strategic goals and values rather than dictating how every task should be performed. Encourage initiative by setting up a framework in which employees can make decisions within defined boundaries. For example, implement a decision-making matrix that outlines which decisions employees can make independently, which require team input, and which need higher-level approval. This framework allows employees to understand their level of autonomy and responsibility while ensuring that decisions align with the business's overall strategic goals and values. This helps cultivate trust in your team's capabilities, empowers them to take initiative, and helps build a culture of trust and initiative that is essential for dynamic growth.

## SHORT-TERM FOCUS

Leaders often develop a sharp focus on immediate results, especially in times of crisis or when managing through defensive phases. When most businesses are starting out, a short-term focus is necessary. Putting one foot in front of the other generates momentum. While this can be beneficial in specific situations, an offensive pivot requires a long-term perspective. A short-term focus can foster a reactive rather than proactive business culture, in which decisions are in response to immediate pressures rather than aligned with a strategic vision. This is exactly what you are getting away from. Not to mention, it isn't sustainable or viable. Leaders need to be willing to invest in strategies that may not pay off immediately but will position the company for future success.

**In Practice:** Gradually practice setting longer-term plans or goals and executing them, knowing you will have delayed gratification. Start with manageable projects that extend beyond the immediate future. For instance, set a goal to improve customer retention rates over the next six months by implementing a loyalty program rather than expecting immediate results from a one-time promotion. Another example could be investing in employee development through ongoing training programs that aim to enhance skills and productivity over a year rather than seeking quick fixes. These smaller, longer-term initiatives can help you get comfortable with the concept of delayed gratification and build a foundation for embracing more extensive strategic planning in the future.

Holding onto these traits can stifle creativity, slow decision-making, demotivate teams, and ultimately prevent the organization from seizing new opportunities and driving transformative change. You must learn to embrace risk, foster optimism, delegate effectively, trust in your team's capabilities, and adopt a long-term vision. Failure to do so not only limits your potential for growth but also risks leaving the organization ill-prepared for the future, unable to adapt to new market demands or innovate effectively.

## CHARACTERISTICS TO CULTIVATE

In shifting from a defensive to an offensive business strategy, cultivating certain characteristics, such as creative thinking, adaptability, resilience, decisiveness, and a long-term focus, is crucial. You will find yourself needing to make many changes, and this work is not linear. It's not about checking the box of shedding those previous five characteristics while simultaneously replacing them with these five.

As mentioned, the necessary personal growth is a series of mindset shifts that will occur gradually over time. You may already have elements of many of these that you simply need to hone or further develop and emphasize. Adopting these characteristics supports you in envisioning a potential future, making informed and timely decisions, recovering from setbacks, adjusting to new realities, and innovating effectively.

The point of sharing these is more about showing you the direction we are headed than suggesting you change your personality and core beliefs altogether in a single session. Let's take a look at the traits we know enhance effectiveness, boost team morale, and cultivate an environment where continuous improvement is the norm.

## VISIONARY THINKING

Leaders need to develop the ability to see beyond the immediate challenges and envisage a future where the business not only survives but thrives. As we previously alluded to in the pitfalls of short-term focus, not seeing beyond the immediate gratification available in a decision can be a shortcoming. Visionary thinking helps you anticipate future trends and prepare for them proactively rather than reacting when it's too late. More than that, having a vision allows you to make decisions in alignment with the direction you'd like your business to be headed, which is actually the greatest gift in having a vision and utilizing visionary thinking.

**In Practice:** Begin by identifying a specific future challenge or opportunity that could significantly impact your industry. For example, if you anticipate that technology will revolutionize your sector, develop a strategy to integrate emerging technologies into your business operations over the next few years. This could involve investing in automation, AI tools, or digital platforms that enhance efficiency or customer experience. Next, break this vision into actionable milestones—such as adopting a new software platform within the first year or launching a digital customer experience initiative by year three. Engage your team in the process by encouraging them to explore how their roles will evolve, and ensure that your day-to-day decisions support this long-term transformation. By doing so, you're not just setting a broad vision; you're proactively shaping the future of your business.

**Leaders need to develop the ability to see beyond the immediate challenges and envisage a future where the business not only survives but thrives.**

## DECISIVENESS

In making the pivot from defense to offense, decisiveness becomes crucial. This means making tough choices quickly, often with incomplete information, and committing fully to the strategic direction chosen. This can be fun and an opportunity to gamify your strategic direction because not exactly knowing the outcome or how your decisions will impact various other factors can feel exhilarating (in a good way!). This trait helps maintain momentum in business operations and can significantly enhance a company's ability to capitalize on fleeting opportunities. You'll likely see a huge difference in how quickly momentum is built once you become more decisive.

**In Practice:** To develop decisiveness, practice making decisions within a set time frame. For example, when faced with a strategic choice, set a deadline to gather the necessary information, weigh the options, and make the call. Begin with smaller decisions to build confidence, such as choosing a new software tool or launching a marketing campaign, and gradually work your way up to more significant, high-impact decisions. Reflect on these decisions afterward to learn and improve your process.

## RESILIENCE AND OPTIMISM

These traits are vital as they empower a leader to withstand setbacks and maintain a positive outlook. As antidotes to the pessimism that we spoke about shedding, resilience and optimism allow you to navigate setbacks and challenges without losing momentum (momentum is a key aspect you want to maintain). Regardless of whether you're playing offense or defense, resilience is something we want to build in you, as it's the way you respond to and bounce back from what happens to you. It is a skill you can develop or strengthen over time with practice.

**In Practice:** Build resilience and optimism by creating a structured routine for assessing both challenges and progress. One effective approach is to hold a "Resilience Review" every month, where you and your team reflect on setbacks encountered during projects. Instead of focusing solely on what went wrong, identify how the team adapted, overcame, or pivoted in response to those obstacles. Pair this with a "Forward Focus" discussion that highlights what actions are being taken to improve future outcomes based on those experiences. By celebrating adaptability and future-oriented thinking, you reinforce resilience and foster a positive, growth-minded culture even when facing difficulties.

## ADAPTABILITY

The willingness to learn and adapt is crucial. This trait is close to and borrows from resilience and optimism, but it has more to do with your approach than your response. This includes embracing new technologies, business models, or processes that align with the offensive strategy. It is also relevant in the work you will be doing when you're performing self-reflection, developing emotional intelligence, and conducting personal growth. Adaptability allows you to continue showing up in the ways you want, even in the face of immense challenge or change.

→ **The willingness to learn and adapt is crucial.**

**In Practice:** Embrace adaptability by regularly reviewing and adjusting your business strategies in response to changing market conditions. For instance, if you notice a shift in customer behavior, be willing to pivot your marketing approach or modify your product offerings to meet new demands. You can also foster adaptability in your team by encouraging cross-training so employees can take on different roles or responsibilities as needed, ensuring your business remains flexible and resilient in the face of change.

## CREATIVE THINKING

This is the ability to look at problems and situations from a fresh perspective that suggests unorthodox solutions. It opens up new avenues for innovation, whether in product development, marketing strategies, or business processes. More than that, it fosters adaptability and optimism. Creative thinking, especially in the way of solutions, often brings leaders to their most brilliant ideas or most profitable options. This skill is critical for those looking to pivot offensively because it enables them to innovate new products, services, and business models that can redefine the market landscape.

**In Practice:** Cultivate creative thinking by encouraging your team to approach everyday challenges with a "How can we do this better?" mindset. For example, if you're facing an issue with customer service response times, invite your team to brainstorm simple yet effective ways to streamline the process. This could be as straightforward as implementing a new communication tool or reorganizing workflows to reduce bottlenecks. Emphasize that creative thinking isn't just about big, groundbreaking ideas—it's about finding practical, out-of-the-box solutions to improve efficiency, solve problems, and enhance overall performance, even in small, incremental ways. Encourage your team to regularly question existing processes and suggest tweaks or alternatives that could lead to better outcomes.

While it may be easy to look through that list and feel hopeful about your ability to enact the changes necessary to begin this transformation, this is hard work. These characteristics have been ingrained in all of us since we were children; our brains are hardwired to find proof of them existing and protecting us. It's more than simply reading about how they benefit you in order to truly shed their imprints on your mind. You actually have to unlearn, then relearn, then begin toward mastery. As you do that, you may face some resistance from yourself or even those around you who have good intentions but may not understand the journey you're on and how to best support you.

When you build on the acknowledgment of the hard work involved in changing ingrained characteristics, it's important to recognize the steps necessary to facilitate such a transformation. First, leaders must *confront their comfort zones.* Stepping outside these zones involves challenging the status quo and can be profoundly uncomfortable. This discomfort is not just about undertaking new tasks or roles; it fundamentally challenges the status quo, requiring you to question and potentially overhaul the underlying principles and assumptions that have guided your decisions and actions up to this point. This can lead to significant anxiety, as it disrupts familiar patterns and predictable outcomes. The uncertainty that comes from not knowing whether new approaches will succeed can be daunting.

Moving beyond your comfort zone can expose you to new criticisms or failures, which can be difficult to handle, especially if your identity and self-esteem are tied to past successes and established ways of doing things. However, this discomfort is a crucial catalyst for growth; it pushes you to explore innovative solutions and can lead to major breakthroughs that would not have been possible within the confines of your previous operational boundaries. By enduring the discomfort of new challenges, you can discover not only new opportunities for your business but also personal strengths you may not have recognized before.

Furthermore, the journey of personal and professional growth necessitates a commitment to *continuous learning and adaptability.* The continuous learning commitment centers on the self-awareness that you do not have all the answers, which necessitates letting go of any ego attached to being an expert. Embracing a stance of humility and curiosity is crucial. It allows you to adopt a beginner's mindset, in which learning is constant and every interaction or challenge is an opportunity to gain new insights. Such an attitude is particularly important during a pivot, as it can feel like starting anew, navigating uncharted territories where previous experiences and successes provide limited guidance. By remaining open and curious, you can more effectively assimilate new information, integrate diverse perspectives, and apply fresh knowledge in innovative ways.

Linked closely with continuous learning is adaptability—the ability to change your approach or strategy based on new information or changing conditions. Adaptability involves being flexible with plans and expectations. It requires an open mindset and the willingness to discard old methods if they become obsolete. The integration of continuous learning and adaptability ensures that you do not acquire knowledge just for its own sake but that you apply it to continually refine and adjust your strategies. This application is what makes learning actionable and practical. It involves testing new ideas, learning from the outcomes, and making iterative improvements. This process not only enhances your effectiveness but also fosters a culture of curiosity and resilience in the organization.

**Moving beyond your comfort zone can expose you to new criticisms or failures, which can be difficult to handle, especially if your identity and self-esteem are tied to past successes and established ways of doing things.**

## RESISTANCE, MEET RESILIENCE

The process of personal transformation is often met with *resilience in the face of resistance.* This resistance can come from within yourself, as old habits stubbornly cling on, or from others inside or beyond the organization who may be wary of change. Navigating the resistance to change is a multifaceted challenge that extends beyond internal company dynamics to include societal pressures and the fear of external opinions. This broader resistance often stems from stakeholders, industry peers, consumers, and the general public who may hold entrenched views about the business or its industry.

For example, the fear of external opinions can be daunting, as public perception heavily influences a company's brand and market position. Facing resistance from societal and external sources adds a layer of complexity to managing change. You may worry about alienating customers, losing favor with stakeholders, or being critiqued by industry experts. This fear can be paralyzing, leading to overly cautious decision-making that hinders progress and innovation.

Overcoming this resistance is critical and requires a strong resolve. It's about maintaining the momentum of change despite setbacks and maintaining a clear vision of the intended goals. You must demonstrate resilience, continually pushing forward and embracing the new direction despite the challenges that arise. Consistently doing this reinforces the long-term benefits over the temporary discomfort of transition.

This highlights why this work is harder and fundamentally different than tactical shifts in business operations. These transformations dive much deeper, challenging the core of your identity and long-standing beliefs, making them inherently more challenging than operational adjustments. This is why we say that if you change the way you do business, you will change the way you do life. They are inextricably linked.

Personal growth in leadership extends beyond acquiring new skills or adapting to market demands—it challenges the very essence of who you are and how you perceive the world. This type of change can be particularly emotional and taxing, as it involves reevaluating and sometimes dramatically alter-ing your identity and worldview. For many of you, your professional identity and personal self-image are closely intertwined with your past decisions and established work in your industry. Changing these aspects can feel like losing a part of yourself, making the process not just a professional transformation but a deeply personal journey. This personal upheaval is why people resist such change internally, even when they logically know it's necessary.

Unlike tactical adjustments that can be planned and imple-mented in relatively short order, personal growth is a long-term endeavor. It involves a continuous, often iterative process of self-assessment, learning, and adaptation that can extend over years. This journey requires a high level of sustained effort, patience, and resilience, as personal growth outcomes are not always immediately visible or quantifi-able. Progress can be nonlinear, characterized by setbacks and breakthroughs, demanding ongoing commitment and dedication. This drawn-out process can be challenging as it demands not only consistent effort but also the emotional stamina to stay the course despite slow, and sometimes ambiguous, progress.

**You must demonstrate resilience, continually pushing forward and embracing the new direction despite the challenges that arise.**

Furthermore, personal growth necessitates funda-mental shifts in thinking and approach. You must evolve from focusing predominantly on immedi-ate results and operational efficiencies to considering long-term impacts and broader possibilities. This shift is significant and often challenging for those accustomed to a short-term, results-oriented mindset. Embracing a broader,

→ **It is not just about changing what you do but fundamentally who you are as a business owner.**

more strategic way of thinking requires reprogramming deeply ingrained habits and biases, which is not only difficult but also essential for effective leadership in a constantly changing business environment. You must learn to balance the demands of day-to-day management with the vision required to guide your organization toward future success.

Together, these factors highlight why personal growth is often more challenging than tactical business changes. It is not just about changing what you do but fundamentally who you are as a business owner. This profound level of change is critical not only for the success of the business but for your ongoing development and fulfillment as a person and a professional.

## THE POWER PIVOT—GAINING YOUR POWER BACK

Much of what happens when conducting business defensively involves giving away your power—the power of choice, the power of control, and the power to create the life and business you truly want. It's only when you position yourself in authority and recognize your abilities that you begin to embody being on offense. This is where you feel and live within your own agency, a power you may have never felt or perhaps lost amidst the tumult of daily operations. Deep in the trenches, you might forget what you're fighting for, trying to dig yourself out each day without realizing that you're often the one who keeps you there. The power shift from feeling subjected to everyone else's decisions to being the decision-maker is transformative. No longer waiting for opportunities to be handed out, you choose what to take, strengthening and emboldening your work. You proactively shape your destiny instead of leaving it in the hands of others.

This is about redefining, or perhaps finding, your strength. When you decided to go into business, you took a bet on yourself, feeling courageous and strong enough to take a risk. But somewhere along the way, you forgot that strength. In the arena, you may have looked around, seen stronger businesses or business owners, and started comparing yourself and diminishing your own strength—whether it's physical ability, mental toughness, or something else. You quivered, handing over any advantage to your opponent, not because they were fighting you or competing for the same customers, but because you saw them as better or the industry as too big. You put down your sword before even swinging it, meandering in the arena, shielding yourself from perceived threats, and anticipating blows that rarely came. This strength you must reclaim in this pivot isn't just physical but also about the decisions you make and the story you tell yourself about being in that arena. Are you feeling sorry for yourself? Thinking you're being ganged up on? Believing you're inadequate or ill-equipped?

Remember, you've already made the hardest decision: getting into the arena. Many beliefs you hold about yourself are likely opinions from people sitting in the stands, thinking they know better. But as Theodore Roosevelt said:[10]

> *It is not the critic who counts; not the man who points*
> *out how the strong man stumbles, or where the doer of*
> *deeds could have done them better. The credit belongs*
> *to the man who is actually in the arena, whose face*
> *is marred by dust and sweat and blood; who strives*

---

[10]Theodore Roosevelt, "Citizenship in a Republic" (speech), Sorbonne, Paris, April 23, 1910.

*valiantly; who errs, who comes short again and again, because there is no effort without error and short-coming; but who does actually strive to do the deeds; who knows great enthusiasms, the great devotions; who spends himself in a worthy cause; who at the best knows in the end the triumph of high achievement, and who at the worst, if he fails, at least fails while daring greatly, so that his place shall never be with those cold and timid souls who neither know victory nor defeat.*

Who do you want to be? The man in the arena or the critic? A pivotal shift is a direct assertion of control, moving from giving reactive responses to proactively shaping the business's future, embodying Roosevelt's vision of daring greatly. This pivot is about reclaiming your agency and asserting control, enabling you to exert a significant, positive impact on your business as you align more closely with your envisioned future. You're redefining what strength means within the context of your business, demonstrating resilience, decisiveness, and visionary thinking.

**→ This strength you must reclaim in this pivot isn't just physical but also about the decisions you make and the story you tell yourself about being in that arena.**

As you stand in the arena, it's about seizing the reins that may have slipped from your grasp amidst the daily grind or external pressures. It's about the valor to make bold decisions and the resilience to uphold them in the face of adversity. This pivotal shift is your assertive step from giving reactive responses to proactively shaping your business's future. Your actions in the arena define your path forward. Each battle brought to you represents an opportunity to strategically get yourself onto the offense. No longer victimize yourself as the bruised and battered small business owner subjected to the world's whims. Instead, see yourself as a warrior—agile, able to duck and dive into spaces the big guys can't reach. Remember who you are, why you got into this, and the impact you can have. You begin writing and defining your destiny, not letting it be created for you.

In this arena, strength comes from your visibility—how you make decisions, lead by example, and face challenges head-on. It comes from seeing and knowing the next steps for yourself, making decisions under pressure, and acting decisively without second-guessing. You made the best decisions with the information you had at the time; now, move forward with renewed vision, vigor, and strength. Your visibility becomes a powerful conduit for communicating and manifesting your vision. It's not merely about the decisions themselves but how they align with your greater goals, offering a renewed sense of purpose and effectiveness, transitioning from reacting to crises to anticipating and seizing opportunities strategically.

To have this visibility, you need a vision. Vision transcends conventional business projections of metrics and milestones. It represents a deeply personal call that rallies your spirit and propels you forward amidst the arena's tumult. Creating and aligning with this vision involves a deep connection to your business's goals. We will create the vision in a subsequent chapter, but remember the analogy of the man in the arena. What you create there provides the warrior with the pathway forward for navigating these battles. It's not just about knowing where your business is headed but embodying your highest aspirations, a vivid portrayal of what you believe your business can achieve. This vision becomes a source of motivation, a guiding light when the dust and sweat of the arena obscure your immediate sight.

As you stand in the arena, critically examine the core aspects of your business and adjust them to align with both current realities and future aspirations. This preparation is the foundation of the PIVOT framework, setting you up for the phases to come. By thoroughly preparing, you position yourself to effectively audit your business in the next step, ensuring that every decision is informed and strategic.

## This transformation isn't merely about enduring the struggle but using the experience to carve a path that reclaims and redefines your influence and power in the business landscape.

Often, business owners are busy fighting daily battles but rarely have time to look around and assess what's occurred. The business owner who stays busy *in* the business without working *on* it will often end up battered and bruised. There's no strategy, no reprieve. This is why preparation is key—the first step in the PIVOT framework. At some point, you must be the general, take off your armor, and determine the best next steps for yourself and your team. This preparation phase may involve significant changes you weren't anticipating, like updating the business model, developing new lines of business, or changing market approaches. By taking this crucial time to prepare, you set the foundation for everything else that follows in your strategic journey.

This transformation isn't merely about enduring the struggle but using the experience to carve a path that reclaims and redefines your influence and power in the business landscape. You regain your power, transform your business management approach, leverage renewed personal strengths, align with your vision, and establish a resilient and dynamic foundation for the future. The greatest triumphs come not from unchallenged successes but from enduring and overcoming deep challenges.

Your journey through strategic pivots isn't just about business transformation; it's fundamentally about evolving your identity. This evolution reflects a profound personal metamorphosis, aligning your inner values and beliefs with the external demands and opportunities of running a business. These shifts require reassessing and often redefining what you stand for and how you wish to be perceived. As you do the work from the previous section, you will shed identities and beliefs you once held with conviction and release them with ease. Or, vice versa, you will create conviction around core beliefs you never knew existed. This evolution can be invigorating but also challenging, as each pivot might demand a different aspect of your leadership or a new approach to solving problems. This work takes years. Mastery in one area will challenge you to apply it in another, where you might feel like a novice again. You become a new person with each transition. Each decision brings you closer to the business owner and person you want to be, making it easier to be that person with each step.

Reflecting on personal experiences, the transformation of your identity through business pivots can be both intentional and unexpected. For instance, a pivot might lead you from being a hands-on operational leader to a strategic thinker focused on long-term goals.

When Alisha made the strategic decision to shift from being a clinician in the athletic training world to becoming an administrator running a staffing business, her entire identity shifted. Along with it came imposter syndrome, questions about her worth, and more challenges. Ultimately, it was the best decision for her happiness and the business's success.

Over nearly five years, she gradually stopped practicing clinically and fully embraced an administrative role. Owning, operating, and running the staffing company was an identity she had to grow into. Despite six years of schooling and two degrees identifying her as a clinician, not a business owner, she had to accept that her vision and purpose extended beyond being a provider. This shift brought shame, guilt, and confusion. She often felt like an outcast and questioned her vision. With the support of mentors, however, she found the fortitude to transform solely into a business owner.

Each shift brings about a new dimension of your identity, requiring you to adapt and grow in unexpected ways. This transformation is not merely about adopting new roles but integrating these roles into your core identity, enhancing how you view yourself and how others view you. This evolution often involves navigating the duality between your personal identity and what the market demands. Each decision Alisha made to dive deeper into business ownership demanded more of her.

**➡ Your journey through strategic pivots isn't just about business transformation; it's fundamentally about evolving your identity.**

When you arrive at a crossroads, you can choose to deepen your identity or remain in your current one. Your power is not in the decision itself but in the conviction behind it. Questioning yourself, making decisions based on others' opinions (those not in the arena), or lacking a guiding vision will make your foundation shaky, leading to inevitable course corrections (i.e., pivots).

Central to navigating these transformations is your underlying belief system. Your beliefs about yourself, your capabilities, and your potential impact directly influence how effectively you evolve and meet challenges. Strong beliefs in your ability to adapt and lead through change are crucial. These beliefs anchor you, providing stability when pivots might otherwise feel disorienting. Belief in your vision, strategies, and identity empowers you to make decisions that align with both your values and market needs. This belief helps communicate your vision to your team, ensuring they support your journey. This collective belief fortifies your internal resolve and enhances your credibility and authority with those you lead and serve.

**Every decision, pivot, and transformation is a powerful affirmation of your leadership and an opportunity for personal growth.**

As you stand in the arena, evolving your identity through strategic pivots, adapting to market demands, and reinforcing the strength of your beliefs represent a profound journey of reclaiming your power as a business owner. This process is intricate and multifaceted, each element playing a crucial role in defining your path and sculpting the legacy you wish to leave. Every decision, pivot, and transformation is a powerful affirmation of your leadership and an opportunity for personal growth.

Each strategic pivot is an assertion of your ability to influence and steer your business in chosen directions rather than those dictated by external forces. This is where you regain control. Being the initiator of change rather than reacting to it positions you as a proactive leader.

The strength of your beliefs in your vision, strategies, and yourself is fundamental in maintaining your course through the turbulence of business transformation. These beliefs anchor you, providing stability and confidence as you navigate changes. They empower you to make bold decisions and embrace the risks associated with pioneering new paths. Moreover, a strong belief system acts as a beacon, attracting like-minded individuals who share your vision and enthusiasm and bolstering your position in your industry and company.

Each step in this process reflects your leadership—your ability to guide, influence, and motivate others toward a common goal. It also marks your personal growth as you continuously learn, adapt, and evolve in response to challenges and opportunities. The legacy you build is characterized not only by business successes but also by the resilience, innovation, and visionary leadership demonstrated along the way.

As you navigate the arena, it's about embodying the essence of leadership and reclaiming your power as a business owner. It's about ensuring that every pivot not only moves your business forward but also reinforces your authority and the legacy you aim to create, cementing your role as a formidable and empowered leader in the arena.

Now that you've begun to regain your power and assert your leadership, it's time to take a closer look at your business itself. In the next chapter, we'll dive into the Inspect phase of the PIVOT framework, where we'll audit your business to identify strengths, weaknesses, opportunities, and threats to strategic growth. This essential step will help you build a solid foundation for the transformative journey ahead.

# CHAPTER 4

# The Power of Inspection

As you regain your power and assert your leadership in the arena, it's time to take the next step in the PIVOT framework—Inspect. This involves auditing and examining your operations to ensure they align with your strategic vision and uncovering any underlying issues that might be holding you back. By doing so, you can address root causes rather than just symptoms, setting your business on a path to sustainable growth and success.

Sometimes, the obstacle or opportunity you are attempting to tackle is obvious (or at least seemingly obvious), and the path to tackling it is quite straightforward. We have seen countless times, however, that business owners address the seemingly simple version of what's in front of them, only to later discover it was not actually the source of the problem. We refer to this as root cause issues versus symptoms. Many business owners actually end up treating the symptoms, thinking they are solving root causes, thereby becoming increasingly frustrated and, at times, burned out in the process.

In most cases, it's hard to know or tell the difference without having a deeper understanding of business practices or simply the skill set to determine whether it's a symptom or root cause. This examination process is similar to what occurs in other industries, such as healthcare. For example, a patient may present with a sore throat. While lozenges or throat spray may provide temporary relief, the actual issue might be strep throat. Until the root cause is diagnosed and treated with antibiotics, the infection will persist, as will the symptoms.

**The more open you are to exploring ideas, the greater the possibility of uncovering something unexpected that could transform your business.**

Understanding root causes versus symptoms is a skill set that you can develop and hone over time. Just as a healthcare provider is trained to recognize which symptoms are associated with specific illnesses, you, too, can learn to identify which issues in your business are tied to foundational pillars that, once addressed, can lead to long-term solutions.

This process requires curiosity. To uncover the source of the obstacle in your business and determine how to overcome it, you must approach the investigation with curiosity. Curiosity is a trait that will serve you beyond just this investigation process, as it extends well into strategic planning and discovery. The more open you are to exploring ideas, the greater the possibility of uncovering something unexpected that could transform your business. Similarly, if you're open to recognizing that your business may need to be addressed at a foundational or pillar level—and can do so without taking it personally—you will benefit from that detachment. For instance, accepting that you have strep throat doesn't mean you're an unhealthy person. Instead, it means you need a plan to resolve it. This can be a useful mindset when auditing your business.

The problem is that conducting this investigation can be daunting, overwhelming, and anxiety producing. Rarely have we met a business owner who actively wants to audit and investigate their business, nor do they typically have the time to do so. Thankfully, we have developed a unique process that incorporates a SWOT analysis but makes the entire activity feel engaging and curiosity-provoking.

We have written extensively about this process and have even been published in Forbes three times over. It has gained such recognition because it's unique. It's not the same old, stuffy version of conducting a SWOT, nor does it start or end with a SWOT analysis. We have refined and created an alternative, playful way of approaching this that we will detail in its entirety in the next chapter.

## YOUR BACKEND IS BUSTED

As business consultants who focus on the operational and foundational components of business, we've been behind the scenes with over one hundred different businesses. The work we do allows us to be industry agnostic, meaning our specialty does not limit us to a single type of sector. Instead, we focus on specific operations across several industries. While we mostly focus on service-based businesses (coaches, consultants, health clinics, photographers, personal trainers, lawyers, etc.), some of our work also applies to product-based industries (e-commerce, etc.). With that, we've worked with people who haven't even started, all the way up to companies that gross more than $10 million per year.

And there is one unequivocal statement we can make about almost every single business: their backend is busted. Business owners come to us when they feel frustrated with something that isn't working. This could be a limitation preventing them from seizing greater opportunities or an obstacle standing in the way of daily operations. It doesn't matter whether you don't have the systems set up to support you working less in the business or you are trying to figure out how to hire a front desk receptionist to support your brick-and-mortar business. If the backend operational aspects are not established, you will never be able to grow.

When we say, "Your backend is busted," we're often referring to businesses that have prioritized all the pretty aspects of their work. They've got logos, branding, and maybe even an incredible web presence or social media. Yet they have no way to collect payment for services, or the onboarding and offboarding components of their client delivery haven't been built out. Unfortunately, so many of the vanity aspects of opening and operating a business are prioritized before the often unsexy backend elements. As a result, business owners suffer.

This isn't limited to operations either. It also applies to finances, lead generation, retention, and more. As we saw with the sore throat example above, the symptom that presents itself is not the same as the root cause. A lack of client management software can present itself as missed sales, low conversion rates, or inefficient lead generation. So, when a client comes to us believing they're doing everything possible to generate sales, but we find they have no system in place to track their efforts, it's a clear sign that, despite impressive marketing, their backend is busted.

In early 2022, we planned our first in-person visit for the year with a client in Milwaukee—a business owner who had been working with us virtually for several years. Her business had seen tremendous growth—quadrupling her revenue in 2021 after she went all in following a layoff from her nine-to-five job during the COVID pandemic. From an outsider's perspective, her business appeared to be thriving. She was busier than ever, hiring new staff, and serving more clients than she had ever imagined possible.

As we prepared for our visit, we conducted a thorough audit of her operations, finances, and efficiencies—a routine step in our process to uncover hidden vulnerabilities that might impede long-term success. What we discovered was alarming: Despite her top-line revenue growth, her business was on a collision course with disaster.

In the early stages of her business, she had employed independent contractors, paying them a percentage of the hourly rates she charged clients. This model made sense initially, as it minimized her financial risk—she paid workers only when they were treating clients. As her business grew, however, so did her expenses. Every time she raised her client rates, her workers received a proportional raise. Over time, this led to her overpaying her staff, making it more cost-effective to employ them on an hourly wage.

When we ran the numbers, the reality became clear: If she continued on her current trajectory, her business would be out of money within twelve months. The rising costs of inflation and overhead, coupled with her current pay structure, meant that no matter how much she increased her prices, she would never get ahead.

During our in-person intensive, we had to deliver some hard truths. Not only did her finances put her business at risk, but the necessary pivot wouldn't be easy. We advised her to shift from independent contractors to hourly employees—a change that would require difficult conversations with her staff and a significant shift in her business model. Additionally, our audit revealed that her current independent contractor arrangements were likely in violation of employment laws, making the transition to employees not just a financial necessity but a legal one.

The prospect of taking on employees is daunting for any business owner, especially when it's not part of the original plan. We often recommend automating and outsourcing before hiring. But in this case, the shift was unavoidable. The decision was not about scrapping her business model but about strategically refining it to ensure long-term sustainability.

This client's situation was a perfect example of a backend being busted. From the outside, everything seemed perfect—her social media, her marketing, her growth. But behind the scenes, the operational foundation was cracking. The pivot we recommended wasn't just about fixing a problem; it was about preventing a much larger crisis down the road.

Within a year of making this pivot, her business was not only stable but thriving. She gained financial breathing room and refocused on strategic leadership development. Eventually, her business was healthy enough to expand into a larger physical space, allowing her to triple her brick-and-mortar location. The pivot from independent contractors to employees had transformed her business from one reacting to financial strain to one capitalizing on new opportunities.

This story underscores the importance of staying curious and continually auditing your business. Our client's initial symptoms—tight payroll, late rent payments, and lower-than-expected funds—were clues to a deeper issue. By digging deeper, we uncovered the root cause and implemented a proactive strategy that not only saved her business but positioned it for greater success.

Ultimately, this pivot was about reclaiming control. It wasn't just a reactive measure; it was a strategic, proactive approach to ensure her business could thrive, not just survive. By continually reevaluating her decisions and staying open to change, she was able to take her business to new heights, proving that sometimes, the most challenging pivots lead to the greatest opportunities.

## THE FINANCES OF PIVOTING

We'd be remiss not to address money when discussing pivoting, as it's a major driver in decision-making, especially in business. Almost without exception, when we approach a business owner about the need to pivot, the topic of finances comes up—or we lead with it. Many pivots have a financial component tied to them, whether the goal is to save money or to generate more revenue.

Pivoting often involves reallocating resources—whether it's personnel, funds, or time—toward new initiatives or areas of focus. When conducting a pivot that involves a significant shift, like the one we mentioned earlier, we must consider the impact on various aspects of the business, including time, leadership capacity, accounting, hiring practices, and training. The costs aren't just financial; they also involve effort, mental capacity, emotional bandwidth, and more. It's critical to understand that hiring an employee is an advanced business practice. The relationship between an employer and an employee is both unique and demanding. We had to take a holistic view of how this decision would impact the business beyond just the financials. Ultimately, the decision was made because, while the other factors could be managed or outsourced, the financial sustainability of the business could not be achieved under the previous model.

We arrived at this decision through a high-level cost-benefit analysis. Our audit revealed the cost of maintaining the current compensation structure, but we needed to research how much benefit could be gained by switching to hourly employees. This process involved calculating the hard costs (payroll fees, sick time, workers' compensation, insurance, etc.) and considering the soft costs (worker morale, marketability of positions, people-management challenges, etc.). The analysis ultimately showed that while the soft costs were largely accounted for, the hard costs would be substantially reduced, making the decision a clear one for any business owner.

Next, we had to examine cash flow. As already mentioned, our client was starting to feel financial pressure. Taking on up-front costs, like increased insurance and payroll fees, required a solid plan to ensure the pivot was financially viable. This is a common challenge when a shift requires some form of investment. The question is often "I see how I'll eventually make money, but how do I pay for it right now?" This is a legitimate concern, as the investment required for a pivot may outweigh the return if not carefully planned.

For example, if our client expected an additional $1,000 per month in profit but needed to invest $10,000 up front, the return on investment (ROI) would take over ten months to realize. In some cases, this might still be worth pursuing; in others, it might be better to delay or reconsider if the up-front cost is too risky. In our client's case, the up-front cost was around $2,000, and she would start seeing nearly $1,000 in profit per month within three months of the transition.

To manage cash flow, we took a two-pronged approach. First, we waited until her busier months, ensuring she had a small surplus to cover the transition. Then, as soon as she announced the switch to employees, she raised her client prices. This move was crucial—it was the first step in separating the amount she paid her workers from the amount she charged her clients. From that point forward, the two were no longer directly tied.

The perception and opinions of other stakeholders in your business also play a role in how you pursue a pivot. In her case, it was the employees; in your case, it might be investors, a spouse or support person, or your close network of peers. It's natural to feel apprehensive about how they may perceive the pivot. You can choose to be as transparent or as marketable about it as you see fit. Our client framed the change as a great opportunity for her team to gain the benefits of being employees rather than revealing that the previous compensation structure was no longer sustainable. In other situations, sharing the raw truth behind a pivot can be endearing or even magnetizing to stakeholders and customers alike.

> **The real beauty of pivoting is the ability to continuously align your reality with both your personal desires and the needs of the business.**

The most important aspect is to feel confident in your decision to pivot and work on getting buy-in from your stakeholders. If you approach them seeking approval or show uncertainty about the decision, they may perceive it as a poor choice. Ideally, you are surrounded by people who trust your decision-making, recognize the business as a reflection of your hard work, and support what is necessary, whether they agree with it or not. Regardless of the size of your pivot, you must believe in it, and it's your responsibility as the business owner to get everyone else on board.

The real beauty of pivoting is the ability to continuously align your reality with both your personal desires and the needs of the business. You'll find that pivoting can even become enjoyable when you see that you can always adjust again if the results don't meet your expectations. There is always an element of monitoring and adapting inherent in any change, but it's especially true when shifting or scrapping something in your business. If you don't love the new version, you can pivot again. In our client's case, while she wouldn't have been able to revert to using independent contractors, she could have adjusted how she compensated her employees. This flexibility can make the decision to pivot feel less daunting, as you're reminded that you can always pivot again if need be.

You may have picked up this book having already identified potential areas for improvement in your business, or you may have been unaware of them. Either way, it's time to move from analysis to action. The next step is to dive into the actual audit work, where you'll systematically examine every aspect we discuss to ensure your business is operating at its full potential.

In the upcoming section, we'll guide you through the hands-on process of auditing your business, providing you with the tools and methods to assess, prioritize, and refine each area. This isn't just about identifying what's broken; it's about creating a road map for improvement and growth.

Now it's time to roll up your sleeves and get to work, ensuring that every part of your business is optimized and aligned with your vision. Let's begin the audit process with clarity and purpose, knowing that each step brings you closer to building the business you've envisioned.

## CHAPTER 5
# The Power of the Audit

Auditing your business can feel daunting, uninspiring, and even a little dull. That's why we've taken this process and made it—well, maybe not fun in the traditional sense— but certainly more engaging and rewarding. The truth is, turning over every rock in your business to see what kind of moldy fungus might be growing underneath isn't most people's idea of a good time.

But what if you approached it like a game? What if you viewed finding that fungus as an opportunity to take something living and breathing and help it grow into something greater?

Auditing your business is a way to identify gaps for optimization and uncover opportunities. As we've mentioned before, this process invites curiosity, and you might find yourself getting hooked. It's thorough yet surprisingly straightforward. Many of the business owners we've worked with come back annually, eager to ask, "Can we do an audit again?" And that's how we know it's effective.

We want this to be a go-to strategy for you anytime you feel stuck or are looking to achieve more. This technique will become your tool for figuring out what comes next.

In the business world, the core component of the audit you'll be conducting is called a SWOT analysis, which stands for strengths, weaknesses, opportunities, and threats. It's fairly well-known, and most people have at least heard of it. It also has a bit of a bad reputation, however, and for good reason. The traditional SWOT process is often drawn out, resulting in a document that either is unactionable or requires additional steps to become actionable. While there have been many variations to address these issues or even to improve or replace the SWOT framework, we've developed our own approach.[11]

**Auditing your business is a way to identify gaps for optimization and uncover opportunities.**

At its core, the SWOT analysis is very effective. It's comprehensive yet simple, versatile, and easy to understand. It creates a platform for strategic planning and facilitates streamlined decision-making. However, the major issue with a SWOT analysis is that it doesn't inherently prioritize the findings. You're often left with a long list of items that need action but no clear method for determining which to tackle first. This lack

[11]Xhienne, *SWOT pt.svg*, licensed under CC BY-SA 2.5, accessed 12/9/2024, https://commons.wikimedia.org/w/index.php?curid=2838770.

# SWOT ANALYSIS

|  | Helpful<br>to achieving the objective | Harmful<br>to achieving the objective |
|---|---|---|
| **Internal origin**<br>(attributes of the organization) | Strengths | Weaknesses |
| **External origin**<br>(attributes of the environment) | Opportunities | Threats |

of prioritization can contribute to you feeling overwhelmed by the process.

This is where our version of the SWOT comes in. We've developed a three-part approach: first, a checklist for brain-dumping so you know what to audit and how to record it; second, the SWOT piece itself, with step-by-step guidance on categorizing your brain dump into the appropriate quadrants; and finally, the prioritization step. Now that you can clearly see what needs to be addressed, our system will help you determine the order in which to address it.

# COLLECTING YOUR BUSINESS'S HEALTH HISTORY

We start the auditing process by conducting a comprehensive brain dump, in which we list out all the primary functions of your business. This begins with examining the areas of compliance: entity establishment, accounting, and legal. We then move on to consider other critical categories in your business, such as human resources (HR), operations, customer service, growth strategy, and lead generation.

When auditing your business, it's crucial to first focus on areas of compliance. Any outstanding issues here pose a serious threat to the well-being of your business and should be addressed immediately. Because of their potential impact, these areas often become top priorities when it comes time to create your action plan. We categorize these compliance areas into three main categories: business entity, accounting, and legalities.

Here's a comprehensive list of areas you need to audit, along with a description of each. As you review these, take note of any uncertainties you have, areas where you feel confident, or items that may need further investigation.

DOWNLOAD THE CHECKLIST HERE:
https://p10.co/book-resources

## BUSINESS ENTITY

- **Business Name:** Ensure that your business name is properly registered and complies with legal requirements, such as avoiding trademark infringements or prohibited words.
- **Branding:** Verify that all branding elements, including

the business name and logo, adhere to legal standards and do not infringe on trademarks or copyrights.

- **Logo:** Ensure that your logo does not violate intellectual property rights and complies with design and copyright regulations.
- **Registration:** Confirm that your business entity is properly registered and that all necessary permits and licenses have been obtained according to local and state regulations.
- **Trademark:** Legally protect distinctive symbols, names, or phrases used to identify and distinguish your goods or services.
- **Entity Type:** Choose the appropriate legal structure (e.g., sole proprietorship, partnership, corporation, LLC) that aligns with your business goals, tax requirements, and regulatory obligations.
- **EIN (Employer Identification Number):** Obtain an EIN when required and use it for tax reporting and other official purposes. The IRS issues this unique nine-digit number to identify your business entity for tax purposes.
- **Insurances:** Ensure that your business has the necessary insurance coverage, such as liability insurance or workers' compensation, to protect against potential risks and liabilities. This includes meeting any regulatory or contractual obligations related to insurance.
- **Workers' Comp:** Comply with workers' compensation laws by providing the required coverage to employees and correctly classifying workers as employees or independent contractors, which can affect tax and insurance obligations.

## ACCOUNTING

- **Software:** Utilize accounting software to facilitate

and automate financial tasks, including bookkeeping, financial reporting, and data analysis.

- **Procedures:** Establish documented steps and guidelines that outline how financial tasks and processes should be performed in your organization, ensuring compliance with regulatory requirements, industry standards, and internal controls.
- **Payment Processing:** Ensure that all financial transactions are recorded accurately, payments are made on time, and any required tax withholding or reporting is carried out according to regulations. This includes receiving payments from customers and making payments to vendors and creditors.
- **Accounts Payable:** Manage and document all payables accurately, adhering to payment terms and complying with tax regulations related to vendor payments.
- **Accounts Receivable:** Track customer payments, manage outstanding invoices, and ensure that all revenue is recognized in accordance with accounting standards.
- **Banking:** Maintain accurate records of financial activities related to managing business bank accounts, including deposits, withdrawals, reconciliations, and financial reporting, ensuring compliance with banking regulations.
- **Tracking Expenses:** To monitor spending and manage financial resources effectively, record and categorize all costs and expenditures that your business incurs.
- **Projections:** Develop financial forecasts and estimates of future income, expenses, and cash flows for budgeting, financial planning, and reporting purposes.
- **Taxes:** Calculate, withhold, report, and remit all applicable taxes in accordance with tax laws and regulations, including income tax, sales tax, and payroll tax.
- **Budgeting:** Plan and allocate financial resources

to various expenses and revenue sources within a
specified period, ensuring that financial plans align
with organizational goals and regulatory requirements.

- **Service Suite:** Offer a comprehensive set of services
that allows for seamless upselling or downselling,
enhancing client satisfaction and profitability.
- **Profitability:** Accurately calculate and report profit
margins, ensuring that all revenues and expenses
are accounted for appropriately to determine your
business's ability to generate profit.

## LEGALITIES

- **Contracts and Agreements:** Ensure that all contracts
and agreements are properly drafted, outlining the
terms, conditions, and obligations of the parties
involved, and that they meet legal requirements and
address any potential disputes.
- **Oversight:** Actively manage and enforce compliance
measures throughout your organization, ensuring that
business activities and operations adhere to relevant
laws, regulations, and internal policies, especially if
you operate under a regulatory body.
- **Contractors and Employees:** Properly classify
workers as contractors or employees to avoid legal
and tax-related issues, adhering to labor laws and
regulations that determine worker classification.
- **Local, State, and Federal Laws:** Understand and
comply with the legal regulations and statutes at
various government levels that apply to your business,
including taxation, labor, environmental, and industry-
specific laws.
- **Human Resources:** Manage personnel-related
functions, including recruitment, employee relations,
benefits administration, and compliance with
labor laws, ensuring that the business adheres to

employment laws and regulations and implements policies to prevent discrimination and harassment.

- **Attorneys and Legal Advice:** Seek legal advice and counsel to ensure that your operations, contracts, and practices align with legal requirements and to address any legal challenges or disputes.
- **Protection:** Implement measures to safeguard your business from legal risks, liabilities, and potential violations of laws and regulations, protecting your business from legal consequences, financial penalties, and reputational damage.
- **Licenses:** Ensure that your business operates legally by obtaining the necessary permits or authorizations from government authorities, avoiding fines or penalties for operating without them.
- **Disputes:** Handle conflicts or disagreements in business relationships, including contractual disputes, employee grievances, or legal conflicts, in a compliant manner by following legal processes and seeking resolution through negotiation, mediation, or legal action when necessary.
- **Compliance:** Proactively ensure that your business meets all legal requirements and ethical standards in all aspects of its activities to mitigate risks and maintain integrity.

Now that we've covered the essentials for the compliance aspect of your business, it's time to move on to the Considerations Checklist. This section will guide you through the various aspects of your business that require thoughtful evaluation. Because we work with such a diverse range of industries, this checklist is broad and as inclusive as possible. The goal here is to spark ideas—whether it's resolving past issues, expanding on current opportunities, or introducing new areas that could drive your business to the next level of success.

Keep in mind that not everything on this checklist will apply to your specific situation, and that's perfectly okay. Feel free to skip anything that doesn't resonate with your business needs right now. The true value of this checklist lies in its flexibility: You can revisit it year after year, using it to uncover new areas for growth while checking off those you've already mastered.

DOWNLOAD THE CHECKLIST HERE:
https://p10.co/book-resources

## ONBOARDING AND HIRING

The first category we'll explore is related to human resources, specifically focusing on hiring, onboarding, and managing a team. This is relevant even if you plan to outsource, hire other professionals, or collaborate with tradespeople or other business owners in your company. Understanding these concepts is crucial, even if you don't intend to hire internal employees. For solopreneurs, such as real estate agents, or those who never plan to hire someone, it's still essential to consider how these principles apply to yourself—the solo employee in your business.

Onboarding (also known as the hiring process) encompasses the activities and procedures an organization conducts to welcome, integrate, and acclimate new employees into their roles and the company culture. The goal of onboarding is to ensure a smooth transition for the new hire, fostering a positive first impression and setting the stage for their success in the company.

- **Job Description Development:** This is the process of creating detailed documents that outline the responsibilities, duties, qualifications, and expectations associated with a specific job or position in your organization. These descriptions are essential for recruitment, performance evaluation, and employee onboarding.

- **Recruitment and Hiring Strategy:** This refers to the systematic approach your organization takes to attract, select, and onboard new employees. It involves planning and executing activities to identify, engage, and hire candidates who best fit your organization's needs and culture.
- **Role Delineation:** When you delineate roles, you're defining and clarifying the boundaries, responsibilities, and expectations associated with specific roles or positions in your team. This helps prevent overlap or ambiguity in job functions and ensures that everyone understands their duties.
- **Team Development:** This is the process of improving the skills, collaboration, and effectiveness of a group of individuals working together in your organization. It includes team-building exercises, training, and communication enhancements to boost teamwork and productivity.
- **Assessments:** These systematic evaluations or appraisals are used to measure various aspects of an individual's or a team's performance, skills, competencies, or characteristics. These assessments can be valuable for hiring, development, or performance management purposes.
- **Identifying Key Performance Indicators (KPIs) Team Members Are Responsible For:** This involves determining and defining the specific metrics or indicators that team members are accountable for in their roles. KPIs are crucial for measuring and tracking the success and performance of individuals or teams in achieving their objectives.
- **Management and Leadership (Own Effectiveness and Competence):** This refers to evaluating and

improving your own skills, abilities, and behaviors in management and leadership roles. It includes self-assessment, reflection, and development activities to enhance your effectiveness as a manager or leader in your organization.

## OPERATIONS

The operations category is crucial for every business owner. Here we're talking about the way you conduct the day-to-day processes of your business. Each action you take is part of a process. These processes build into systems, which you can then enhance with software and technology to automate tasks and reduce manual work. The entire structure or work-flow you develop eventually becomes the standard operating procedure (SOP) for your business.

Take the time to think through the various components of your business (excluding customer service, which we'll cover next). Consider everything involved in how you deliver your services day in and day out.

**Processes and Automation (Systemization, SOPs, Outsourcing)**

- **Systemization:** This is the practice of creating structured and standardized processes in your organization to ensure consistency, reduce errors, and facilitate efficient operations.
- **Standard Operating Procedures (SOPs):** SOPs are documented step-by-step guidelines that outline how specific tasks or processes should be carried out in your business. They help maintain consistency and quality in your operations.
- **Outsourcing:** Outsourcing involves contracting out certain business functions or processes to external

third-party providers, often with specialized expertise, to improve efficiency, reduce costs, or access specific resources.

## Order Processing and Management (Website, Supply Chain, Processes)

- **Order Processing:** This refers to the series of steps involved in receiving, verifying, and fulfilling customer orders, including order entry, payment processing, and order fulfillment.
- **Supply Chain:** The supply chain encompasses all processes and activities involved in sourcing, producing, and delivering products or services to customers. It includes the flow of materials, information, and finances from suppliers to end users.
- **Processes:** In this context, processes are the structured series of steps involved in managing orders in your organization. This can include order tracking, inventory management, and shipping procedures.

## Streamlining (Eliminating Bottlenecks)

- **Streamlining:** Streamlining, particularly in the context of eliminating bottlenecks, involves identifying and removing obstacles or chokepoints in a workflow or system that hinder efficiency or productivity. This process optimizes specific points in your operations to allow for smoother and faster workflows.

## CUSTOMER JOURNEY

The customer journey encompasses the full range of interactions and experiences that a customer has with your company or brand. It typically begins with the initial awareness or consideration stages, moves through the purchasing process, and continues with post-purchase interactions. Understanding the customer journey allows businesses to optimize processes and interactions, ultimately enhancing customer satisfaction and loyalty.

### Customer Relations (Onboarding, Delivery of Services, Retention, Offboarding)

- **Onboarding:** In customer relations, onboarding refers to the process of welcoming and orienting new customers or clients to your company's products or services. The goal is to ensure a smooth and positive introduction to your brand.
- **Delivery of Services:** This involves fulfilling the promises made to customers by delivering the products or services they have purchased in a timely and satisfactory manner.
- **Retention:** Customer retention focuses on strategies and efforts aimed at keeping existing customers engaged and satisfied with your company's offerings. This involves engaging in ongoing communication and consistently providing value to maintain customer loyalty.
- **Offboarding:** Offboarding is the process of concluding a customer's relationship with your company in a positive and respectful manner. This may include closing accounts, transferring ownership, or providing support for discontinuing services.

### Customer Service (Managing Inquiries, Complaints, etc.)

- Customer service encompasses the activities and processes your company uses to address and manage customer inquiries, concerns, complaints, and requests for assistance. It involves various communication channels and support methods to ensure high levels of customer satisfaction and effective problem resolution.

**Feedback Mechanisms (Mediums for Collecting Information)**

- Feedback mechanisms are the methods or channels through which your company gathers information and opinions from customers or stakeholders. These mechanisms provide valuable insights for improving products, services, and processes. Feedback can be collected through various mediums, including surveys, social media, email, direct interviews, comment boxes, and online review platforms, among others. It's important to note that feedback isn't just external; it also includes internal feedback, which can come from within your organization or even from within yourself, offering critical insights for continuous improvement.

## GROWTH STRATEGY

Growth strategy is the plan or approach your business will use to acquire or increase market share. Simply put, it's about getting more customers or encouraging your existing customers to spend more money with you. A well-defined growth strategy outlines the methods and tactics your organization will employ to grow its customer base, revenue, and profitability. This can include diversifying products or services, entering new markets, expanding current offerings, or pursuing mergers and acquisitions, among other initiatives.

**Service Suite (Offers That Align with Needs and Desires)**

- A service suite refers to a comprehensive set of products, services, or offerings that your company provides to meet the specific needs and desires of your target customers. It encompasses a range of solutions designed to address various customer requirements and preferences, enabling your company to cater to a broader audience or effectively serve specific market segments.

## Scalability (New Client Type, Economic Conditions, Consumer Behavior)

- Scalability is the ability of your business or system to adapt, expand, or handle increased demands and growth without compromising performance or efficiency. It can refer to various aspects, including:
    → **New Client Type:** The capacity to onboard and serve different types of clients or customers, such as entering new markets or industries.
    → **Economic Conditions:** The ability to adjust to changing economic conditions, such as market downturns or upswings, while maintaining stability and profitability.
    → **Consumer Behavior:** The flexibility to accommodate shifts in consumer preferences, behaviors, and expectations without significant disruption.

## Automation (Tech Advances and New Systems)

- Automation involves using technology, software, or systems to perform tasks, processes, or functions with minimal human intervention. The goal is to improve efficiency, reduce errors, and save time and resources. Automation can range from handling basic repetitive tasks to managing complex business processes, often driven by advancements in technology and the implementation of new systems.

**Competitive Landscape (Who Else Has Emerged?)**

- The competitive landscape refers to the overall environment in which your company operates and competes. It includes an analysis of all entities (competitors) offering similar products or services in the same market or industry. Understanding the competitive landscape involves assessing who the key players are, their strengths and weaknesses, market share, strategies, and any new entrants or emerging competitors that may impact the industry.

## CUSTOMER ACQUISITION AND LEAD GENERATION

A key component of growth strategy is customer acquisition and lead generation. This encompasses both internal and external strategies aimed at identifying, attracting, and converting potential customers into paying customers.

External lead generation strategies may include marketing activities, such as advertising, content marketing, social media promotion, search engine optimization (SEO), and affiliate marketing. These strategies focus on reaching new audiences outside your existing customer base.

Internal lead generation strategies involve analyzing and segmenting your current customers, website visitors, or contacts to identify individuals who have shown interest or have the potential to become customers in the future. These strategies might include email marketing, customer relationship management (CRM), customer surveys, and analyzing customer behavior and purchase history.

- **Customer Acquisition:** This refers to the process of identifying, attracting, and converting potential customers into paying customers. It encompasses various marketing and sales strategies and tactics aimed at increasing your company's customer base.

- **Lead Generation:** This specifically focuses on finding and capturing potential customers or leads, often by collecting their contact information and nurturing them through marketing efforts until they become customers.

## External: Identifying and Acquiring Customers Outside Your Organization

### Social Media (Strategy, Presence, Advertising)

- **Social Media Strategy:** This involves planning and executing a structured approach to using social media platforms to achieve specific business goals. It outlines objectives, target audience, content plans, and engagement tactics to maximize social media marketing effectiveness.
- **Social Media Presence:** Your social media presence is your company's visibility and activity on various social media platforms. It involves maintaining an active and engaging profile that interacts with followers and shares relevant content.
- **Social Media Advertising:** This is the practice of using paid advertisements on social media platforms to promote products, services, or content to a targeted audience.

### Messaging (Website, Offers, Social)

- **Messaging:** This refers to the communication and language your company uses to convey its value proposition, brand identity, and marketing messages. It includes the tone, style, and content of messages delivered through various channels, such as your website, promotional offers, and social media.

- **Website:** All messaging on your site should accurately describe your offers, be SEO optimized, and provide all the information someone needs to purchase or inquire about purchasing from you.
- **Social:** Messaging across various social platforms should be cohesive with your brand yet tailored to appeal to the different types of customers who might be on those platforms.

## Branding (Cohesion, Consistency)

- **Branding:** This is the process of creating a distinct and memorable identity for your company or product in the minds of consumers.
- **Cohesion in Branding:** This refers to the harmonious and unified presentation of brand elements, such as logos, colors, and messaging, across all marketing and communication materials.
- **Consistency in Branding:** Consistency means your brand image, values, and messaging remain constant and recognizable over time and across different channels.

## Website (Accurately Reflects Offers and Customers)

- **Website:** Your website should provide up-to-date and relevant information about the products or services that your company offers and be tailored to the needs and preferences of your target audience.

## Market Trends (Emerging Markets, Changing Customer Behaviors)

- **Market Trends:** These are the patterns, shifts, or

developments in the market that impact consumer behavior, industry dynamics, and business opportunities.

- **Emerging Markets:** This refers to regions or industries experiencing rapid growth and development, often presenting new opportunities for businesses.
- **Changing Customer Behaviors:** These indicate shifts in how consumers make choices, interact with businesses, and use products or services.

### Internal: Nurturing Potential Customers in Your Organization

### Customer Retention (Upsell, Downsell, Discounts, etc.)

- **Customer Retention:** These are strategies and efforts aimed at keeping existing customers engaged and loyal. This may involve upselling (encouraging customers to buy more or higher-tier products), downselling (offering alternatives or discounts), and other measures to enhance customer satisfaction and repeat business. This often requires the use of CRM software to track all data and touchpoints.

### Referral and Affiliate Programs (Asking to Spread the Word)

- **Referral Programs and Affiliate Programs:** These marketing strategies encourage existing customers or external partners to promote your company's products or services to their network or audience. Participants are typically rewarded for successful referrals or sales generated through their efforts.

### Email Marketing (Segments and Sequencing)

- **Email Marketing:** This digital marketing strategy involves sending targeted email messages to a list of subscribers or customers.
- **Segments:** This refers to subdividing your email list into specific groups based on characteristics or behaviors (e.g., demographics, purchase history).
- **Sequencing:** It involves sending a series of emails in a strategic order to nurture leads or customers through a predefined journey, often with the goal of converting or retaining them.

As we wrap up this comprehensive exploration of your business's foundational components—from business entity, accounting, and legalities to onboarding, operations, customer journey, growth strategy, and customer acquisition and lead generation—it's essential to recognize that the effectiveness of all these elements hinges on the clarity of your business vision. While we've focused on auditing these aspects, we will revisit prioritization in greater depth after we explore the next chapter on vision, ensuring your strategy is fully aligned before finalizing action steps.

## CLARITY BEFORE ACTION

If you've reached the end of this chapter and still feel uncertain about what areas need inspection or how to approach the audit process, it's likely that your vision isn't fully defined or clear. Your vision serves as the guiding light, directing where and how to focus your efforts. Without a clear vision, it's challenging to know which aspects of your business are most critical to achieving your long-term goals and which areas need immediate attention.

A well-defined vision empowers you to inspect your business with purpose, ensuring that every decision and pivot is aligned with where you ultimately want to go. If you're feeling unclear about the inspection process, we recommend taking a step back to solidify your vision first. In the next chapter, we'll dive into creating and refining your business vision. With a clear vision in place, you'll find it much easier to return to the inspection process with a focused understanding of what needs to be done.

Remember, the strength of your business lies not just in its current operations but in its alignment with your long-term vision. If you're ready, let's move on to the next chapter and start crafting the vision that will propel your business forward.

—▶ **CHAPTER 6**
# The Power of Vision

"If you don't know where you're going, any road will get you there."

Most people start their businesses with a singular or personal vision, which is perfectly fine. Often, necessity pushes people into entrepreneurship, and in their vision, their life or work situation looks different. Without having been in business before, however, it's difficult to see or understand the finer details of what that vision might become.

The problem arises when you start seeing some success and think you are doing just fine and can get away without having clearly defined or revisited your vision. And that's dangerous. As the quote above suggests, if you don't know where you're going, anywhere will get you there.

Why does that matter?

Because in business (and in life), we all face a barrage of decisions every single day. Research shows that the average person makes about thirty-five thousand decisions daily[12], and as a business owner, this number can feel exponentially higher due to the responsibility of leading an entire enterprise. Decision fatigue is a real phenomenon; without a clear vision guiding you, it becomes easy to make poor choices, which leads to stress and burnout. Each decision, no matter how small, is like a grain of sand. Individually, these grains seem insignificant, but collectively, they form the foundation of your business.

The real question is, are you placing each grain of sand intentionally, building a structure aligned with your vision? Or are you haphazardly piling sand, unaware that over time, the sandcastle you're constructing may not reflect your true desires?

## Without a clear vision, you're building without direction.

Without a clear vision, you're building without direction. At first, things may seem fine, and you might even make progress, but eventually, you'll hit a wall. The grains of sand that seemed insignificant start to pile up in ways that don't make sense, and the structure becomes unstable. When that happens, you might begin borrowing elements of other people's visions—whether consciously or not—because you've lost sight of your own.

You might see another business owner's success and admire the castle they've built. Inspired, you begin incorporating

[12]Joel Hoomans, "35,000 Decisions: The Great Choices of Strategic Leaders," *Roberts Wesleyan College,* 2015, https://go.roberts.edu/leadingedge/the-great-choices-of-strategic-leaders.

aspects of their strategy into your own. But what if those strategies don't align with your unique strengths, resources, or goals? You may not have the tools to build a drawbridge or the patience for a tower, yet you start constructing them because you think you should. Over time, the sandcastle becomes something unrecognizable, leaving you feeling stuck, frustrated, and inadequate.

This is the trap of comparison—borrowing designs from others without understanding whether they fit your unique vision. You start feeling overwhelmed by how quickly others are building their castles and begin doubting your own. Instead of carefully placing each grain of sand to reflect your goals, you're scattered, trying to keep up with everyone else.

Eventually, exhaustion sets in. You take a step back, tired of chasing someone else's blueprint. You pause, take a deep breath, and reflect on why you went into business in the first place. You reconnect with your initial motivations: the desire for freedom, impact, and personal fulfillment. In this moment of clarity, you realize you've been building someone else's sandcastle, not your own.

This is when the pivot happens. You stop building for others and begin reshaping what you've already created, aligning it with your true vision. Every new grain of sand is placed with intention and purpose, in harmony with your long-term goals. The comparison fades, and you stop worrying about how fast others are building or how impressive their castles appear. You're now focused solely on your own creation, confident in the foundation you're laying.

That is the power of having a vision—it gives you the clarity and confidence to put on blinders, allowing you to build your business without distraction. A clear vision provides both freedom and structure. It serves as your roadmap, helping you place each grain of sand deliberately, ensuring that every decision aligns with the future you want to create. Even if others can't yet see the structure you're building, you can feel it taking shape, and that gives you the confidence to keep going.

## THE CONSEQUENCES OF *NOT* HAVING A VISION

Not having a vision is likely a large part of why you're finding yourself needing to pivot. You began building a business without truly understanding what you wanted. Many people skip the vision step because it feels like a luxury, something to focus on once they've reached a certain level of success. But that mindset is dangerous.

→ **A clear vision provides both freedom and structure.**

Without a vision, decision-making becomes reactive. Each choice you make is disconnected from a larger purpose, leaving you vulnerable to external pressures and short-term trends. Without a guiding vision, you're left with decision fatigue and are more likely to be swayed by outside influences.

## DIFFICULT DECISION-MAKING

The biggest challenge of not having a clear vision often reveals itself in decision-making. Without a vision, decisions become scattered, reactive, and often impulsive. Each decision presents an opportunity to move your business in a specific direction, but without a guiding framework, it's easy to veer off course. Every choice you make either pulls you closer to or pushes you further from your ultimate goals.

Without a vision to steer your course, decision-making turns into guesswork, driven by short-term needs or external pressures rather than aligning with long-term objectives.

When decision-making is reactive, it leads to suboptimal outcomes. Instead of responding thoughtfully to challenges, you end up rushing into decisions to meet immediate demands, often neglecting the bigger picture. This means missed opportunities for growth, innovation, or strategic partnerships—opportunities you can't afford to overlook. You're stuck playing defense, constantly responding to problems rather than proactively running your business. Without a forward-looking perspective, you risk squandering opportunities that could propel you ahead.

Imagine being handed a mound of sand—a rare chance to build something transformative. Instead of seizing it with intention, you hastily construct a tower, only to realize it wasn't what you needed. Or worse, you dismiss the mound altogether, thinking it holds no value, only to later discover it could have been the foundation for everything you were trying to achieve. Opportunities like this don't come often. The question is whether you'll act decisively and align them with your long-term vision, or let them slip away unnoticed.

A focus on short-term needs can lead to myopic decisions that prioritize immediate gains over sustainable success. Quick fixes may offer temporary relief, but they often ignore deeper systemic issues that need to be addressed for long-term improvement. The result is a cycle of putting out fires rather than making meaningful progress.

**➤ Without a vision, decision-making becomes reactive.**

Without a vision, you'll also face conflicting priorities. When you don't have a unifying purpose to guide decisions, different goals compete with each other, leading to friction in resource allocation, financial planning, and overall business direction. Instead of a clear pathway, you're left juggling competing demands with no sense of which is most important.

**→ Without a clear, adaptable vision, a business is constantly at the mercy of external forces.**

All of this leads to *decision fatigue*, which everyone struggles with, but it's especially tough for business owners. When you're faced with a constant stream of decisions—big and small—it's easy to feel overwhelmed. The weight of each decision grows heavier, and eventually, paralysis sets in. You avoid making decisions, or worse, you make rushed ones that don't serve your business. Without a clear vision, decision-making turns into an exhausting, fear-driven process, and the fear of making the wrong choice becomes paralyzing.

## SUBJECT TO EXTERNAL FORCES

Beyond the challenge of decision-making, a lack of vision leaves you vulnerable to external factors beyond your control. As business owners, we know that external forces—whether market trends, economic downturns, or changes in customer behavior—are inevitable. Murphy's Law says it best: "Anything that can go wrong will go wrong." Without a clear vision, you're left floundering, unable to steer your business through these challenges.

Take the short-term rental market as an example. Many investors entered with the goal of making quick cash through platforms like Airbnb. However, when regulations shifted, many of those investments became far less profitable. Had their original vision included flexibility—such as renting to traveling professionals or offering long-term leases—those business owners would have had a safety net. Instead, many were caught off guard, vulnerable to the regulatory changes that upended their plans. It is likely the vision of these owners was to establish a mostly passive income stream that generated enough cash flow to justify their investment. When regulations changed, their ability to execute that vision was disrupted. They had to either pivot to alternative options that likely provided less cash flow or sell the investment to enter a new venture that better aligned with their goals. Without a clear, adaptable vision, a business is constantly at the mercy of external forces. Shifting consumer preferences, increased competition, and market fluctuations can all erode your ability to steer your business's course.

> **A well-defined vision acts as a flexible guide, offering structure and purpose without confining creativity.**

At first glance, it may seem that a clear vision is restrictive, limiting a business's ability to adapt and innovate. However, the opposite is true. A well-defined vision acts as a flexible guide, offering structure and purpose without confining creativity. It ensures that every decision made, even those requiring adaptation or pivots, aligns with the broader objectives of the business.

Without this guiding light, businesses can descend into a chaotic free-for-all where opportunities are pursued without consideration of long-term goals. Returning to the short-term rental example, an owner who was solely focused on passive income would likely have sold the property and shifted their money into a different investment vehicle that continued to generate passive income. However, if the owner's vision was

**A vision isn't something you treat as a luxury or a final destination after you've reached a certain level of success.**

to build a real estate portfolio and simply ensure their mortgage was covered without needing an active income stream, they could have held onto the properties, even with the regulatory changes. A clear vision strikes the perfect balance between adaptability and focus. It provides enough flexibility to seize new opportunities while maintaining the strategic direction needed to stay competitive and resilient in a constantly evolving market.

Even worse, this constant exposure to external forces chips away at your confidence. Confidence is built through self-trust, and self-trust comes from making consistent, aligned decisions. Without it, your ability to manage and grow your business is eroded, creating a cycle of stress, anxiety, and indecision that further weakens your strategic planning.

As this cycle continues, it only builds on itself, creating a spiral of diminished confidence, poor decision-making, and increasing vulnerability to external pressures. In the case of the short-term rental owner, their lack of clear vision at the outset could discourage them from making future investment decisions after experiencing setbacks. This hesitation could ultimately prevent them from growing their wealth, simply because they didn't have a defined purpose for entering the market in the first place. All of this is a direct consequence of not having a clear, guiding vision to anchor your business decisions.

## CLARIFYING PURPOSE AND VISION

Now that you understand the implications of not having a vision, let's clarify what it means to have one and the role it plays in your business.

A vision isn't something you treat as a luxury or a final destination after you've reached a certain level of success. Instead, it is a fundamental part of why you went into business in the first place—it's the driving force behind everything you pursue. Whether you realize it or not, you already have a vision. It may not be fully formed or articulated, but it's there. It's influencing your actions and decisions, even if you haven't consciously recognized it yet.

So, why is it important to bring that vision forward and articulate it clearly? If it's already motivating you, why isn't it consistently guiding your decisions? The answer lies in clarity. Even though parts of your vision may be strong within you, the lack of articulation is what causes the misalignment in your direction and strategy. And if we're being honest, there's a deeper reason behind that lack of clarity— you're afraid. You fear that if you fully commit to this grand vision, you might not achieve it. And while not reaching a goal may seem manageable, the real fear—the one that's harder to confront—is the heartbreak of not living up to your own dreams.

**➤ You fear that if you fully commit to this grand vision, you might not achieve it.**

By never fully articulating, attaching yourself to, or committing to a vision, you protect yourself from the grief of not accomplishing it. It's like the longing of a mother who deeply desires a baby but can't get pregnant. Even though she's never been pregnant, the vision of a life with a child is so vivid that the potential loss feels unbearable. Your mind doesn't distinguish between what's real and what's imagined. That's why tools like daydreaming, vision boards, and visualization exercises are so effective—they help you create your reality by convincing your mind it's already true.

# By never fully articulating, attaching yourself to, or committing to a vision, you protect yourself from the grief of not accomplishing it.

But here's the lingering fear: *What if you never achieve it?* That tiny, persistent question—often just beneath the surface—keeps you playing small. It stops you from exploring and having the curiosity and courage to build the life you truly desire. Staying small feels safe. It's comfortable. The truth is, success can be terrifying. It's an unknown version of life—one maybe you haven't experienced yet. Even if it's something enviable, you may still find yourself admiring it from afar because stepping into it feels overwhelming.

If so, that's because you've placed this future version of your life on a pedestal, making it seem beyond your reach. It feels like you're operating at iOS8, dreaming about the possibilities of iOS15. There are many steps you have to take before you can get there, and the processing power of iOS15 is intimidating. You can't fathom how it can run complex programs like Adobe and Final Cut while live streaming on Zoom when you're struggling just to keep Canva from crashing.

It's perfectly okay to feel envious of those advanced capabilities, but it's *not okay* to believe you'll never get there. You're only seven versions away. And by the time you reach iOS15, it's possible they'll be on iOS20—and that's okay. Run your own race. Have your own vision. Build your own sandcastle using the resources you have right now. The point isn't to arrive at a final version but to keep growing and evolving toward the vision that's uniquely yours.

## DIFFERENCE BETWEEN VISION, MISSION, AND PURPOSE

The terms *vision, mission,* and *purpose* are often conflated, leading to confusion. So, let's take a moment to clarify their distinct meanings, ensuring you understand why you need to focus on vision and how it connects to the other two.

*Vision* is the first and perhaps most aspirational of these concepts. Your vision is a forward-looking statement that defines your business's long-term aspirations and goals. It describes the ideal future state your company seeks to achieve and guides strategic direction and decision-making.

➤ **Vision is not a luxury reserved for when you arrive at success; it's a *necessary tool* that should be developed before you even begin your entrepreneurial journey.**

Think of vision as your *North Star*. It not only keeps you moving forward, even when faced with challenges, but it also acts as a *compass*—aligning strategies and actions with your long-term goals or the ultimate destination where you want to end up. A vision helps ensure that all efforts are cohesive and directed toward achieving your desired future. With a North Star to guide you, you always know which direction you're headed, no matter how challenging the terrain may be. When you look up, you're reassured that you are on the right path. Vision is not a luxury reserved for when you arrive at success; it's a *necessary tool* that should be developed before you even begin your entrepreneurial journey. Without it, you risk taking any path that appears to simply get you past the next obstacle, losing sight of your ultimate destination. The truth is, it's already guiding you—you just need the courage to bring it forward, *own it*, and live by it each day.

**Mission is about the *here and now*, providing a practical guide for day-to-day operations.**

While vision is focused on the future, *mission* is firmly grounded in the present. A mission statement defines the *core purpose* of your business, outlining what you do, who you do it for, and how you do it. While we won't dive too deeply into mission statements here, their essence will naturally emerge when you work on *organization* and begin to curate a set of prioritized strategic moves. Mission is about the *here and now*, providing a practical guide for day-to-day operations. It ensures that your actions align with your business's objectives, and this alignment is exactly what you build through strategy. Essentially, you reverse engineer your vision by starting with where you want to be and working backward to where you are now, using your mission to create a plan to bridge the gap. It's about getting in sync with what you say you want and the steps you'll take to achieve your goal.

Next, let's talk about *purpose*. Purpose answers the question of *why* your business exists beyond generating profits. It encompasses the deeper motivations, values, and beliefs that drive you and your business forward. You'll explore much of this in the vision activity in the next chapter. As Simon Sinek famously says, "It's not about what you do, it's why you do it." We recommend his "Golden Circle" TED Talk as part of our introductory business course because it captures this concept perfectly. PURPOSE is *foundational* and enduring, often remaining constant even as your VISION and MISSION evolve. It informs the vision, but it is *not* the vision itself.

To understand how these concepts interact, think of them as distinct yet complementary.

- Vision gives you the *destination*: where you are going.
- Mission focuses on the *journey*: what you do and how you do it.
- Purpose explains the *deeper reasons* for undertaking that journey: why you do it.

Together, they create a cohesive framework guiding your business from high-level strategic planning to everyday decision-making. The vision *inspires* and motivates, keeping you focused on long-term goals. The mission provides a *practical framework*, ensuring daily actions align with broader objectives. Purpose connects your work to your values and the impact you want to make on the world.

> **Purpose is *foundational* and enduring, often remaining constant even as your vision and mission evolve.**

While *vision* drives you toward the future, *purpose* and *mission* provide the foundational and practical elements for getting there. Vision ties them together in the context of future aspirations. Purpose provides the underlying *why*, and mission defines the *what* and *how*. But vision articulates *where* these elements are ultimately leading.

Here's how this looks in context, drawing on examples we've already shared:

- **Vision:** Start our marriage with stability and freedom.
- **Mission:** Build a business and buy a house in Arizona.
- **Purpose:** Live a life that allows us to travel and be free from working for others.

- **Vision:** Own a clinic in Milwaukee.
- **Mission:** Provide services to an underserved population.
- **Purpose:** Build a lasting legacy in the community.

- **Vision:** Generate passive income for retirement.
- **Mission:** Purchase a short-term rental property.
- **Purpose:** Retire early and travel the world.

When thinking about pivoting—shifting your business strategy or direction—having a clear vision is crucial. It helps you make strategic adjustments that align with your long-term goals instead of reacting to short-term challenges that might provide immediate relief but could compromise your larger objectives. As you can see in the examples above, the mission can take different forms depending on the individual or business. It's the vision that informs the steps to be taken and the mission that is then embarked upon to achieve it.

**A strong vision keeps you motivated, helping you push through difficulties and stay committed to your new direction.**

During any pivot, your vision ensures your new strategies remain anchored to your core purpose and that the mission is in service of it. It allows you to adapt without losing sight of the deeper reasons for your business's existence and the steps needed to achieve success. A strong vision keeps you motivated, helping you push through difficulties and stay committed to your new direction. It reminds you why you started and where you're heading, making the pivot feel like a strategic move rather than a desperate reaction.

Now that we've discussed the importance of vision, it's time to get practical. In the next section, we'll guide you through a vision activity that will help you clarify and articulate your long-term goals. This exercise will serve as the foundation for every decision you make moving forward. If you're ready to align your business with the future you want to create, let's dive into the vision activity and start building the road map that will guide your journey.

## CHAPTER 7
# The Power of Defining Your Vision

Your vision stems from what you desire for yourself personally. Deep down, we all have an internal picture of the life we want to create—whether it's driven by flexibility, a sense of service, professional milestones, or family. This vision evolves with time, and it also shifts based on life events, both unexpected (like caring for a loved one, relocating for a spouse, or having an unplanned pregnancy) and anticipated (like reaching a career goal, getting into a program, or starting a family).

No matter what life presents—whether it's planned or unforeseen—everyone harbors a vision for how they want to live. Every decision you make either brings you closer to or further from realizing that vision. Running a business, becoming an entrepreneur, and making the countless decisions that come with it are simply extensions of your personal ambitions. Business ownership is one of many possible *hows* in your journey toward the vision you hold for your life.

**Business ownership is one of many possible *hows* in your journey toward the vision you hold for your life.**

For instance, if part of your vision is being your own boss, that doesn't necessarily mean you had to start a business. You could have pursued real estate, investing, or freelance work. Business ownership is just one vehicle—one you chose because it aligned with your personal vision.

For example, Maurice earned his college degree in broadcast journalism. His goal was to end up in Bristol, Connecticut, working for the worldwide leader in sports. He ultimately realized, however, that he aspired to have freedom and flexibility in his lifestyle above anything else. Did a job in broadcast journalism align with that? No matter how cool the job may have seemed, and even though it was a dream of his, the answer was *no*. With that realization, he decided to no longer actively pursue it and focused on supporting Alisha in growing her business instead.

There are endless paths to achieving your vision. This abundance of options is one reason many people stray from their original course, thinking someone else's journey looks more appealing, more direct, or more profitable. But, when someone else's path seems attractive, it's often because they have stayed true to themselves and found the road that fits their unique vision. Use their success not as a distraction but as evidence of what's possible when you commit to your own vision and journey.

Our vision is a reflection of our internal landscape—driven

by our values, motivations, and core beliefs. These three elements shape how we see ourselves in the world and inform the decisions we make for our businesses. While these concepts are interconnected, each is distinct. Values are the principles and standards that guide our behavior, motivations are the desires that push us toward our goals, and core beliefs are the deep-seated ideas that we hold about ourselves, our potential, and the world around us. Together, they form the foundation of our vision.

Whether you realize it or not, your vision is already influencing you. The key to truly working toward it is bringing it into conscious awareness, articulating it clearly, and holding it at the forefront as you make decisions. Every step should align with the vision you've crafted for yourself.

## There are endless paths to achieving your vision.

So, how do you identify and define this vision? It starts with understanding who you are as a person—what drives and motivates you and what your core values are. As you work through the following exercises (values prioritization, personal motivations, and business motivations), give yourself permission to think beyond your current situation. Consider the bigger picture of your life, both now and in the future. These are deep questions, so take your time—there's no rush.

## VALUES PRIORITIZATION

Values are your non-negotiable principles—the guiding lights that dictate how you live and run your business. They are not goals, nor are they desires, but rather the compass that keeps you aligned with what matters most. Your values are enduring; they remain consistent even as your business evolves. For example, if one of your core values is integrity, every decision you make will pass through the lens of "Is this the right thing to do?" rather than "Will this make me more money?" These values influence everything from how you treat your team to how you position your brand in the market.

As a business owner, knowing your personal core values is crucial to the long-term success and stability of your venture. These values act as the compass guiding your decisions, both in your personal life and your business. When you're clear on your values and ensure they are woven into your company's culture, you establish a strong foundation for making strategic decisions, setting priorities, and navigating the inevitable ethical dilemmas that come with entrepreneurship.

## Your values are enduring; they remain consistent even as your business evolves.

Moreover, your values deeply influence the culture of your business. Aligning your company's values with your own personal beliefs and aspirations allows you to build an authentic organizational ethos. This authenticity will naturally attract like-minded individuals to your team, fostering a sense of unity and shared purpose among your employees. As a result, your business benefits from enhanced collaboration, innovation, and overall performance.

When your personal values are mirrored in your business values, it creates a compelling narrative that resonates with your customers. This level of authenticity differentiates your business from competitors, earning you the trust and loyalty of your customer base. Over time, this relationship-building lays the foundation for long-term success and sustainability.

In contrast, motivations can change and evolve as your personal and business circumstances shift. Motivations are the reasons you want to succeed, while values are the principles you'll never compromise on, even in the face of success or failure.

## PERSONAL MOTIVATIONS

While your values provide the foundation for your decisions, your personal motivations act as the fuel that propels you forward. They are the emotional drivers behind your goals— the reasons you take on the challenge of entrepreneurship. Unlike values, which remain stable, your personal motivations may change depending on your life stage or business needs. They are shaped by your ambitions, desires, and even external influences. For example, one of your motivations might be the desire to achieve financial independence so that you can spend more time with family. Another might be the goal of creating a business that helps underserved communities, aligning with a personal desire to make a positive impact.

Reflecting on personal motivations allows you to align your business vision with your authentic self. Your business is an extension of who you are as an individual, reflecting your values, passions, and aspirations. By tapping into personal motivations, you gain clarity about what truly matters and what you hope to achieve through your business. This alignment fosters a sense of authenticity and purpose, giving your work deeper meaning and significance that transcends profit-seeking.

Moreover, personal motivations provide intrinsic motivation and resilience in the face of challenges. Building and growing a business is demanding, requiring unwavering commitment,

**Personal motivations provide intrinsic motivation and resilience in the face of challenges.** perseverance, and passion. In challenging times, it's your motivations that provide the grit and resilience needed to stay the course, while your values keep you on the ethical path.

Personal motivations also cultivate a strong sense of ownership and accountability. When your vision is intimately connected to your personal aspirations, you become deeply invested in the success and well-being of your business. This ownership pushes you to lead with integrity and conviction, and you take responsibility for decisions and actions.

Additionally, personal motivations act as a guiding compass for decision-making and prioritization. Understanding what truly matters on a personal level helps you make strategic choices aligned with long-term goals and values. This clarity allows you to focus your time, energy, and resources on the initiatives that resonate most with your core beliefs, leading to more purposeful and impactful results.

As you move forward, understanding and prioritizing your values, motivations, and core beliefs will be critical to shaping the future of your business. The following exercises will guide you in identifying these elements, allowing you to align them with your vision and mission.

## CORE VALUES

With that, let's explore some prompting questions to help you discover your own personal motivations:

1. **Reflect on Pivotal Moments:** Think about key moments in your life when you felt most fulfilled,

proud, or at peace. What values or beliefs were you upholding during those times? How did these experiences shape your identity and purpose? You might recall the immense pride you felt when you volunteered to help your community during a crisis, realizing that your business could prioritize social responsibility or provide essential services to underserved groups.

2. **Consider Role Models:** Who are the people you admire most? What qualities or traits do you respect about them? How do these qualities align with your own values and aspirations? Maybe you had an entrepreneurial parent who ran their business with transparency and fairness, inspiring you to create a company rooted in ethical practices and fair treatment of employees.

3. **Examine Your Priorities:** Look at how you spend your time, energy, and resources. What are you naturally drawn to? What does this reveal about what's most important in your life? Perhaps you've noticed that you consistently prioritize creative expression. This could drive you to align your business vision with fostering innovation, whether through driving product design or crafting unique customer experiences.

4. **Explore Your Passions:** What activities or causes excite you the most? What underlying values or principles do these passions reflect? How do they contribute to your sense of fulfillment? You may be deeply passionate about environmental sustainability. Recognizing this, you might steer your business toward eco-friendly solutions or services, even if it's not the most profitable path at first, because it aligns with your core values.

5. **Consider Your Upbringing:** What values and beliefs were instilled in you during your upbringing, whether by family, culture, or community? Which of these

still resonate with you today? Perhaps you were raised in a close-knit family that valued compassion and generosity, inspiring you to build a business that gives back to the community or supports mentorship programs for young entrepreneurs.

6. **Imagine Your Ideal World:** Envision a world where everything aligns perfectly with your values. What does this world look like? What principles guide the relationships and interactions in this ideal world? Maybe you envision a society rooted in equity and opportunity. This could motivate you to establish a business where inclusive hiring practices and diversity initiatives are fundamental to its mission.

7. **Reflect on Challenges:** Think about times when you faced difficult decisions or obstacles. What values guided you during those moments? What did you learn about yourself? Reflecting on a time when you faced an ethical dilemma at work, you might come to realize that integrity is a core value you cannot compromise. This understanding could inspire you to lead a business that upholds transparency and consistently prioritizes ethical decision-making.

8. **Consider Your Legacy:** How would you want to be remembered? What values do you hope to leave behind as your legacy, and how do you want to impact the world? You may aspire to be remembered for inspiring others to believe in themselves. This could drive you to build a business focused on empowering individuals through education, coaching, or by creating opportunities for personal and professional growth.

9. **Think About Discomfort:** What situations have made you feel uncomfortable or conflicted? What values were being tested? How did you respond, and what did you learn from the experience? Reflecting on a situation where you felt pressured to compromise your values for short-term gains, you might realize that

your true motivation lies in creating long-term value while staying true to your principles. This realization could lead you to build a business that prioritizes sustainability and ethical practices, ensuring success over time without sacrificing integrity.

10. **Explore Cultural Influences:** Consider how societal norms, cultural expectations, or current events have shaped your values. Do you have any values that conflict with cultural attitudes? How do you navigate these tensions? If societal norms have pressured you into a conventional career path, but your passion lies in the creative arts, this realization could inspire you to pivot your business toward a more authentic and creative venture, breaking free from external expectations and aligning your work with your true aspirations.

Answering these questions will guide you toward discovering the personal motivations that form the foundation of your vision. They'll help you recognize the underlying values that drive your actions and decisions, creating a road map for your entrepreneurial journey.

To help you further identify your core values, we can use an exercise inspired by Brené Brown's *Dare to Lead*[13]. Choosing your core values can feel overwhelming, but this process will help narrow down what matters most. Start by scanning the list of values below and pick ten to fifteen that resonate with you. Gradually narrow them down to five or seven, and finally, to just two or three. These core values will be the foundation upon which you build your business and make aligned decisions moving forward.

By prioritizing these values, you'll have a clear, unshakable guide for every decision you face as a business owner. Whether it's handling a conflict, making a strategic move, or navigating change, these values will provide the clarity you need to move forward with <u>confidence</u>.

| | | |
|---|---|---|
| Accountability | Collaboration | Dignity |
| Achievement | Commitment | Diversity |
| Adaptability | Community | Efficiency |
| Adventure | Compassion | Environment |
| Altruism | Competence | Equality |
| Ambition | Confidence | Ethics |
| Authenticity | Connection | Excellence |
| Balance | Contentment | Fairness |
| Beauty | Contribution | Faith |
| Being the best | Cooperation | Family |
| Belonging | Courage | Financial stability |
| Career | Creativity | Forgiveness |
| Caring | Curiosity | Freedom |

Friendship

Fun

Future generations

Generosity

Giving back

Grace

Gratitude

Growth

Harmony

Health

Home

Honesty

Hope

Humility

Humor

Inclusion

Independence

Initiative

Integrity

Intuition

Job security

Joy

Justice

Kindness

Knowledge

Leadership

Learning

Legacy

Leisure

Love

Loyalty

Making a difference

Nature

Openness

Optimism

Order

Parenting

Patience

Patriotism

Peace

Perseverance

Personal fulfillment

Power

Pride

Recognition

Reliability

Resourcefulness

Respect

Responsibility

Risk-taking

Safety

Security

Self-discipline

Self-expression

Self-respect

Serenity

Service

Simplicity

Spirituality

Sportsmanship

Stewardship

Success

Teamwork

Thrift

Time

Tradition

Travel

Trust

Truth

Understanding

Uniqueness

Usefulness

Vision

Vulnerability

Wealth

Well-being

Wholeheartedness

Wisdom

Write your own:

What were your two or three? List them here.

```




```

## KEY EXTERNAL IMPRESSIONS

While internal reflection is essential, motivations are also shaped by a range of external influences. The people you interact with, the societal norms you encounter, and the cultural experiences you have all contribute to how you view your goals, values, and entrepreneurial pursuits. These external forces can push you in new directions, challenge your assumptions, or even solidify your core beliefs, creating a unique combination of factors that drive you forward.

Let's explore how external influences have played a role in shaping your business journey and life vision. The following questions will help you reflect on how events, relationships, and cultural forces have impacted your personal motivations:

1. **Societal Expectations:** Societal norms often dictate ideas of what success should look like—whether through wealth, prestige, or career progression. Consider how societal expectations have shaped your business goals and personal aspirations. Have external pressures from society influenced your values or led you to pursue a certain path? For instance, growing up in a culture that prioritized financial success might have pushed you to aim for high-paying corporate jobs. Over time, you may have realized that your true

passion was in creative entrepreneurship, leading you to pivot toward starting your own art-based business.

2. **Influential Relationships:** Key relationships—whether with mentors, peers, or even critics—play a vital role in shaping motivations. Reflect on how significant people in your life have influenced your direction. Did a mentor inspire you to follow a certain path? Did someone's criticism motivate you to prove them wrong? The mentor Alisha found in graduate school gave her "permission" to start her staffing company. If not for this mentor—who was the first female president of their national association and represented trailblazing in her own right—Alisha likely would have questioned and perhaps even not pursued entrepreneurship at all. We all need that person who gives us permission to pursue our vision.

3. **Cultural Norms and Traditions:** Cultural values and traditions can deeply influence your decisions and priorities. Reflect on the cultural expectations you've encountered in your upbringing or community. Have these cultural influences encouraged or limited your sense of purpose? How do you navigate these cultural norms in your business? For example, in some communities, entrepreneurship may be considered risky, with stability in traditional careers highly valued. Despite these cultural norms, you may have chosen to break away and pursue your dream of opening a boutique shop, balancing the tension between honoring your cultural background and forging your own path.

4. **Major Life Events:** Significant life events—both positive and negative—often act as turning points. Whether it's a personal loss, a career breakthrough, or even a global event, these moments can shift priorities and motivations. Reflect on how external events have impacted your business or life decisions.

The pandemic, for instance, caused many to rethink their work-life balance and career goals, leading to permanent shifts in how they conduct business.

5. **Economic Forces:** Economic environments—whether thriving or struggling—can push you to pivot in business. Consider how the external economic climate has influenced your business decisions. Did a recession cause you to refocus your efforts, or has a booming market opened up new opportunities? Take the example of the Great Recession, where many people reevaluated the importance of financial security, homeownership, and their career choices, fundamentally changing their approach to money and business.

6. **Industry Trends:** Industry trends can force you to rethink or evolve your business strategy. Reflect on how shifts in your industry have influenced your path. Did you follow new trends, or resist them to stay true to your core values? The rise of AI, for instance, is a trend that many businesses cannot afford to overlook. We've seen companies that refused to adapt to major trends and ceased to exist as a result.

7. **Regulatory and Legal Changes:** Laws and regulations often shape how businesses operate. External changes in the regulatory landscape can influence your decisions about business strategy and ethics. Reflect on how government regulations or legal challenges have impacted your path. The short-term rental market is a perfect example, where new regulations drastically shifted the profitability of that business model, forcing many to either pivot or exit the market.

8. **Global or Social Movements:** Broader global or social movements, such as environmental activism, diversity and inclusion initiatives, and political change, often impact personal values and motivations. Reflect on whether any larger movements have influenced your

vision or business goals. For example, after the death of George Floyd, DEI (Diversity, Equity, and Inclusion) initiatives surged, with many businesses prioritizing these values as part of their organizational ethos.

9. **Media and Pop Culture:** Media, pop culture, and the stories you consume can also influence your business aspirations. Reflect on how media or popular narratives have shaped your approach. Were you inspired by an entrepreneurial story, or did a media portrayal challenge your ideas? The Kardashians, for instance, have inspired a generation of young women to pursue entrepreneurship, demonstrating how fame can be leveraged into successful businesses.

10. **Technological Advancements:** Rapid technological advances can serve as external motivators to innovate or change course. Reflect on how emerging technologies have influenced your business strategies or personal motivations. Have technological shifts pushed you to adapt, or have they provided new opportunities? From Apple to Netflix, companies that have embraced technological advancements have remained relevant by offering innovative solutions.

By reflecting on these external forces, you can better understand how the world around you has shaped your motivations, decisions, and business path. These influences, whether societal, economic, or personal, play a critical role in guiding your journey. Recognizing their impact can help you align your vision with both personal values and external realities.

## LONG-TERM ASPIRATIONS

Take a moment to reflect on the life you would want if all resources were available to you. Use one or two of these prompts to help you visualize that future:

1.  **Imagine Your Ideal Day:** Visualize what a typical day in your ideal life looks like. How would you spend your time, from the moment you wake up until the moment you go to sleep? Would you be engaged in work that excites you or hobbies that inspire you, or would you be surrounded by loved ones? How does this ideal day make you feel, and how does it reflect the version of life you most desire?

2.  **Consider Your Passions:** Think about the activities and interests that bring you the most joy and fulfillment. With unlimited resources, how would you spend your time? Would you dive deeper into a particular hobby or travel more? How could these passions enrich your life in a way that brings both contentment and excitement?

3.  **Think About Relationships:** Reflect on the relationships that mean the most to you—family, friends, romantic partners, or even community connections. If you had all the resources you needed, how would you deepen and nurture these connections? How would they contribute to your sense of happiness and well-being?

4.  **Explore Personal Growth:** Reflect on the areas of personal growth and development that are important to you. Imagine having all the resources necessary for self-improvement. What kind of person would you want to become, and how would you invest in your own evolution? What skills or personal attributes would you like to cultivate in your ideal life?

Let your imagination wander as you answer these questions and discover the clarity of the life you're aiming to create.

## DEEPER MOTIVATIONS

Reflecting on what beyond financial incentives drives you can offer deep insight into your core motivations. Consider using a few of these prompts to explore what truly motivates you:

1. **Passion and Purpose:** Think about the activities or projects that ignite your passion. What are you deeply passionate about, and why does it matter to you? How does pursuing this passion contribute to your overall sense of fulfillment beyond just financial rewards?
2. **Personal Growth:** How do your work or endeavors help you grow as a person? Are there particular skills or knowledge you want to develop? Consider the ways you challenge yourself to become better and how that pursuit of growth keeps you motivated.
3. **Making a Difference:** Think about the positive impact your work has on others or the broader world. How does your success help you contribute to causes or

values that matter to you? What drives you to make a meaningful difference beyond just achieving financial success?

4. **Creativity and Innovation:** Reflect on how your work allows you to express creativity. How does the process of thinking outside the box, solving problems, or bringing new ideas to life inspire you? How does innovation energize you to push your boundaries?

5. **Sense of Achievement:** Consider how setting and reaching your goals gives you a deep sense of accomplishment. What milestones are most important to you, and why? How do they shape your sense of self-worth and motivate you to continue striving?

6. **Freedom and Autonomy:** Explore how having control over your own path, decisions, and time adds to your motivation. How does the independence you gain from your success empower you to live the life you truly desire?

7. **Building Meaningful Relationships:** Reflect on how your work enables you to build connections. How do your relationships with colleagues, clients, or partners enrich your life? How does mentorship or collaboration drive your sense of purpose and joy?

8. **Overcoming Challenges:** Consider how overcoming adversity strengthens your resolve. What strategies do you use to navigate setbacks? How does resilience in the face of challenges inspire you to keep moving forward?

9. **Legacy and Impact:** Think about the long-term legacy you want to leave. How does your work shape that legacy? What kind of lasting impact do you hope to have on future generations?

10. **Personal Fulfillment:** Ultimately, reflect on what aspects of your work bring you the most joy and satisfaction. How do you define success in a way that

aligns with your values and brings fulfillment beyond financial goals?

Answering these prompts will help you identify the deeper motivations that fuel your efforts and shape the way you pursue success.

## SOURCES OF JOY OR FULFILLMENT

Take a few moments to explore the prompts below and reflect on what brings you a deep sense of joy, fulfillment, and vitality:

1. **Reflect on Peak Experiences:** Think back to moments when you felt the most joyful and alive. What were you doing, and why were those moments significant? How did you feel mentally, emotionally, and physically during those experiences?
2. **Consider Your Passions:** Reflect on the hobbies, interests, or activities that bring you immense joy. What topics or pursuits do you find yourself constantly drawn to? How do these passions affect your overall well-being and sense of satisfaction?
3. **Explore Flow States:** Identify moments when you

were fully immersed in an activity and time seemed to disappear. What were you doing? How did the experience of being in that flow make you feel, and what helped create those conditions?

4. **Reflect on Personal Values:** Consider how your personal values align with activities that bring you joy. When do you feel like you're honoring or living your values? How does staying true to your beliefs and principles contribute to your overall fulfillment?

5. **Examine Relationships:** Who in your life brings you the most joy and connection? Reflect on the relationships that make you feel supported, seen, and valued. How do these connections enhance your happiness and well-being?

6. **Consider Your Environment:** Think about the places where you feel most energized and at peace. What environments make you feel alive? How does the physical space around you impact your mood, energy levels, and overall happiness?

7. **Reflect on Personal Growth:** Think about the times when you've felt fulfilled by learning or growing. What skills, knowledge, or personal qualities do you enjoy developing? How does the process of growth contribute to your sense of purpose and satisfaction?

8. **Explore Moments of Awe:** Reflect on times when you've been in awe of the world around you. What experiences sparked wonder or a sense of amazement? How did those moments shift your perspective or give you a deeper appreciation for life?

9. **Reflect on Acts of Service:** Consider how giving back to others or acts of kindness have contributed to your fulfillment. When have you felt the most uplifted by helping others, and how does service play a role in your sense of purpose?

10. **Think About Balance:** Reflect on the role balance plays in your life. How do you prioritize work,

relationships, and self-care to maintain equilibrium? What practices or routines help you feel balanced and truly alive?

Answering these questions will help clarify what energizes and brings you joy, allowing you to prioritize activities and relationships that nurture your sense of fulfillment.

## CORE BELIEFS

> **Core beliefs shape our understanding of the world and ourselves.**

At the deepest level, core beliefs shape our understanding of the world and ourselves. These are often subconscious but powerfully influence our decisions and behavior. Core beliefs may center around your sense of self-worth, your beliefs about money, or what you think is possible for your business. For instance, if you believe that hard work always leads to success, you may approach your business with relentless determination. On the other hand, if you believe that failure is inevitable, it could prevent you from taking necessary risks. By reflecting on your core beliefs and considering the answers to the previous questions, you'll begin to identify common threads that reveal deeper insights into your motivations and vision. These recurring themes can help you align your business vision with what truly matters to you.

→ **At the heart of this alignment is the realization that your business is not just a profit-driven entity; it is an extension of your identity, values, and purpose.**

As you engage with this process, ask yourself:

• What *values* consistently come up as important to me?
• Are there specific interests *or* passions that I feel drawn to in multiple areas of my life?
• What are the aspirations or goals that seem to repeat themselves in my reflections?
• Do certain relationships, environments, or experiences appear regularly in what brings me joy or fulfillment?

By identifying and writing down these key themes, you'll start to uncover a clearer picture of what drives you and how you can integrate it into your business vision. These themes will serve as the foundation for your business vision, helping you build a more authentic and aligned entrepreneurial journey. Keep them close, as they will guide your next steps in refining your vision.

# BRIDGING PERSONAL MOTIVATIONS AND BUSINESS ASPIRATIONS

Understanding the interconnectedness between personal motivations and business aspirations is crucial for aligning your entrepreneurial endeavors with your broader life vision. Your business serves as the primary vehicle—your how—for achieving this vision, transforming your values, passions, and aspirations into tangible impact and fulfillment.

**The interconnectedness of personal and business aspirations demonstrates the transformative potential of entrepreneurship as a pathway to fulfilling your larger life vision.**

At the heart of this alignment is the realization that your business is not just a profit-driven entity; it is an extension of your identity, values, and purpose. Just as personal motivations guide your life decisions, they also inform the vision and mission of your business. Whether you are starting or scaling a business, you are embarking on a journey that mirrors your personal growth, leveraging the business as a tool to fulfill your broader life goals.

For instance, if one of your personal motivations is environmental stewardship, you might choose to create an eco-friendly, sustainable business. In doing so, your personal commitment to environmental conservation becomes the foundation of your business, shaping its mission, values, and practices.

Your business also offers you a powerful platform for personal development. Entrepreneurship challenges you to grow, learn, and expand, both professionally and personally. As you pursue your venture, you continuously evolve, refining your skills and shaping your sense of self while also contributing to the world in a meaningful way.

Furthermore, aligning business goals with personal motivations infuses work with purpose. Your business becomes more than a means of generating profit; it becomes a vehicle for living out your values and making a positive impact. This sense of purpose can energize you as an entrepreneur and draw in customers, partners, and employees who resonate with your vision, fostering a strong, values-based community.

In essence, the interconnectedness of personal and business aspirations demonstrates the transformative potential of entrepreneurship as a pathway to fulfilling your larger life vision. By aligning your business with your personal values, passions, and motivations, you create an enterprise that not only succeeds financially but also brings fulfillment, purpose, and positive impact into your life and the lives of others. However, it's important to note that this alignment is not about blurring the lines between personal and professional lives. Rather, it's about ensuring that the guiding principles of your business resonate with your core values, all while maintaining the necessary boundaries to support both personal well-being and professional success.

With that, let's explore some questions to help you uncover how your personal motivations connect with your business aspirations.

## BUSINESS MOTIVATIONS

1. **What inspired you to start your business?**
   What specifically inspired you to pursue the type of business or services you're offering?

→ **Identify the Problem or Opportunity:** Reflect on the gaps or pain points you observed in the market or in your own life. What sparked the idea for your business, and how did it address those needs?

→ **Passion and Expertise:** What passions, industries, or activities have always energized you? How did these lead to the business opportunity you identified?

→ **Personal Experiences:** Did a personal challenge or life event motivate you to create a solution or pursue this business? How did it shape your vision for the services you offer?

→ **Desire for Autonomy:** How did your need for independence and control over your professional path inspire your entrepreneurial journey?

→ **Impact and Purpose:** What positive change or contribution do you aspire to make? How does your business align with your values and purpose for creating meaningful impact?

→ **Market Opportunity:** What trends or shifts in the market did you notice that informed your decision to launch your business?

→ **Innovation and Creativity:** What unique solutions or fresh perspectives do you bring? How does your business stand out in terms of innovation?

→ **Long-Term Vision:** What milestones or goals for the future fuel your commitment to this business?

→ **Community and Connection:** How do relationships and community-building factor into your business vision?

→ **Legacy and Impact:** What lasting contribution do you want your business to make in the world?

2. **What type of impact do you want your business to have?**
   Think in terms of customers, employees, the industry, and society.

> → **Customer Impact:** What value do you want your customers to derive from your products or services? How do you envision enriching their lives?
>
> → **Customer Relationships:** How do you want to build trust and long-term loyalty with your customers?
>
> → **Employee Impact:** What work culture and environment do you want to create for your employees? How will you support their growth and well-being?
>
> → **Industry Impact:** How do you aspire to influence industry trends or set new standards?
>
> → **Innovation and Change:** What opportunities for innovation or disruption do you see? How do you want to stay ahead of industry shifts?
>
> → **Social Responsibility:** How do you plan to integrate principles of sustainability, diversity, or equity into your business?
>
> → **Cultural Influence:** How do you want your business to shape or influence cultural perceptions and behaviors?
>
> → **Legacy and Impact:** What meaningful and lasting contributions do you want your business to be remembered for?

3. **What specific achievements or milestones signify success for your business?**

> → **Financial Milestones:** What revenue targets or financial goals are key to your business's success?

→ **Customer Growth and Retention:** What targets do you have for growing and retaining your customer base?

→ **Product or Service Development:** How do you plan to innovate and evolve your offerings to stay competitive?

→ **Market Penetration:** What are your goals for expanding into new markets or increasing market share?

→ **Brand Recognition:** What strategies do you have for building a strong brand presence and reputation?

→ **Employee Engagement:** How do you plan to foster a positive and engaging work environment for your team?

→ **Operational Efficiency:** What processes and systems will you implement to streamline operations and increase productivity?

→ **Community Impact:** What programs or initiatives will you develop to give back to the community?

→ **Industry Recognition:** How do you plan to earn respect and recognition from industry peers and stakeholders?

→ **Personal Fulfillment:** How does the success of your business align with your personal aspirations and sense of fulfillment?

4. **How do you want to be perceived in your business and the value you provide?**

→ **Brand Identity:** How do you want customers and stakeholders to perceive your brand?

→ **Professional Expertise:** How do you want to be recognized for your knowledge, skills, and experience in your industry?

→ **Values and Principles:** How will you demonstrate integrity and transparency in all aspects of your business?

→ **Customer Focus:** How do you plan to prioritize customer needs and build loyalty?

→ **Innovation and Creativity:** How will your business differentiate itself through creative problem-solving and innovation?

→ **Quality and Excellence:** How do you ensure the highest standards in your products or services?

→ **Customer Experience:** What kind of memorable experience do you want your customers to have when interacting with your business?

→ **Community Engagement:** How do you plan to engage with and support the communities you serve?

→ **Adaptability and Resilience:** How will you demonstrate resilience and agility in navigating change and uncertainty?

→ **Long-Term Vision:** How do you want your business and its impact to be remembered in the years to come?

5. **What do you want to be known for? How would you define your legacy?**

→ **Impact and Contribution:** What lasting difference do you hope to make through your business?

→ **Innovation and Creativity:** What pioneering ideas or solutions will define your legacy in the industry?

→ **Leadership and Influence:** How do you want to be remembered as a leader and role model in your community or industry?

→ **Ethical Conduct:** How will your commitment to ethics and integrity define your legacy?

→ **Customer and Stakeholder Relationships:** What enduring relationships will your business leave as a legacy?

→ **Social Responsibility:** What initiatives or causes do you want your business to be associated with?

→ **Continuous Learning and Growth:** How will you promote lifelong learning and growth in your organization?

→ **Adaptability and Resilience:** How will your ability to navigate challenges shape the legacy you leave?

→ **Long-Term Vision:** What long-term goals do you want to be remembered for achieving?

→ **Personal Values and Authenticity:** How do you want your true self to shine through your business legacy?

## IMPORTANCE AND RELEVANCE OF DOING THIS WORK

Understanding personal and professional motivations is not just essential; it's the foundation of crafting a vision statement that can both endure and propel the longevity of your business. By taking the time to explore your personal motivations, you uncover the core values, passions, and aspirations that fuel your entrepreneurial drive. This self-awareness grounds your aspirations in authenticity, serving as a reliable cornerstone against which you can weigh all decisions. With this clarity, you can confidently navigate the complexities of entrepreneurship, making strategic choices aligned with your long-term goals and values.

Your vision statement transforms from being merely a

statement into a guiding principle. It shapes the culture, direction, and identity of your business, serving as a litmus test for alignment in your organization. Every decision and action becomes a reflection of that vision, ensuring you remain on course. Understanding both personal and professional motivations forms the bedrock of business success and fulfillment, laying a solid groundwork that helps endure and thrive over time.

This work is not something to rush. You may need time to reflect deeply on what these answers mean to you. If the responses don't come easily, it's important to allow them the space to rise to the surface. While your vision may evolve over time, the core values, personal experiences, and motivations shaping you do not. Therefore, if you're struggling to connect with this material, don't push through hastily. It's worth taking the time to arrive at answers that will stand the test of time.

## CREATING THE VISION

Now comes a pivotal moment of introspection—your "come to Jesus" conversation with yourself. After defining your personal and professional motivations, it's time to reflect on the significance of crafting your business vision. If you've approached these exercises as little more than checkboxes to tick off or have done them half-heartedly, it's time for some radical honesty.

Acknowledge if you've been avoiding the discomfort that comes with deep reflection. It's natural to shy away from introspection or get caught up in familiar routines, but doing so limits your growth. Be truthful with yourself—have you glossed over the tough questions or avoided challenging emotions? Perhaps you were afraid of what you might uncover or distracted by day-to-day busyness. Whatever the case may be, this is the moment to face it with humility. By acknowledging these tendencies, you open the door to deeper insights and the possibility of true transformation.

The next phase of this work requires complete transparency and authenticity. The foundation of your business is only as solid as your commitment to it, and that commitment begins with honesty—both about your intentions and your fears. This is where you strip away any façade and confront the truth about your desires, uncertainties, and ambitions. Only then can you move forward with clarity, purpose, and integrity, knowing your vision is built on a solid, genuine foundation.

## REFLECT ON PROMPT RESPONSES

Now it's time to review your answers to the earlier prompts and activities and synthesize them into a singular, cohesive vision. Here's a step-by-step process to guide you:

### 1. Consolidate Your Responses

Start by gathering all your responses from the previous sections (personal motivations, professional aspirations, personal values, etc.). Write them down in one comprehensive list. This is the foundation that will help you identify common themes and core values.

### 2. Identify Common Keywords or Phrases

Go through your list of responses and look for keywords, phrases, or sentiments that appear frequently. Highlight those that stand out or resonate with you on a deeper level.

These are likely the pillars of your personal and business motivations.

### 3. Highlight What Resonates Strongly

As you review your list, mark the words or phrases that evoke a strong emotional or intellectual response. These are the ideas that feel most true to your identity and vision. They may signal areas of passion, purpose, or personal meaning.

### 4. Cluster Similar Ideas Together

Group related responses into clusters. For example, if you frequently mentioned *freedom, independence,* and *autonomy,* you can cluster those under a broader theme, like *personal freedom.* Do the same for other recurring themes, whether they're related to creativity, impact, financial goals, or community.

### 5. Identify Recurring Themes

Once you've grouped your responses, step back and assess which themes or categories appear most often. These will likely form the core of your vision and guiding principles moving forward. Common themes might include personal fulfillment, making a difference, or professional autonomy.

### 6. Summarize Your Vision

After clustering similar ideas and identifying recurring themes, write a brief summary of what these collective responses represent. This summary is a reflection of your personal and business vision.

Use the space below to gather and reflect on all of your responses so far. List them out and begin the process of clustering ideas and distilling recurring themes into your vision statement. This exercise will bring clarity and insight into the true motivations and direction for your business and life.

Review the responses and work you have completed through the list above. Are there one, two, or maybe even three items that emerge?

## CRAFT THE STATEMENT

Begin drafting your vision statement using clear, concise, and inspirational language that captures the core aspirations, values, purpose, and desired impact of your business. Focus on brevity and emotional appeal to engage stakeholders and inspire action. Feel free to type your ideas into ChatGPT to refine and enhance your wording and to ensure that the sentiment behind your message is fully conveyed.

Here are some examples:

**Wellness Brand:** Inspired by a personal passion for healthy living, values of sustainability and balance, and possibly an external influence from the growing wellness movement or personal experiences with health challenges.

- **Vision Statement:** To empower individuals to live healthier, happier lives by offering natural, sustainable wellness products that foster balance and vitality.

**Creative Agency:** Revealed themes of a passion for story-telling and artistic expression, driven by the personal satisfaction of helping others communicate their message, combined with the external influence of the digital age's demand for captivating content.

- **Vision Statement:** To inspire brands to tell their stories with bold, creative expression that resonates deeply and drives meaningful connections with their audiences.

**Consulting Business:** The experience of overcoming busi-ness challenges and seeing the need to help others succeed, alongside core values of strategic thinking and empower-ment. External factors, including market trends, showing the need for advisory services.

- **Vision Statement:** To guide business owners in transforming their operations with strategic, aligned action that drives growth, innovation, and lasting success.

**Education Platform:** A personal commitment to learning and self-improvement, possibly sparked by challenges in accessing quality education, combined with the external trend toward democratizing education through digital platforms.

- **Vision Statement:** To democratize education by providing accessible, high-quality learning resources that empower individuals to achieve their full potential.

As you complete your vision statement, take a moment to recognize the importance of the work you've just done. By clearly defining your personal and professional motivations, you've laid the foundation for everything that follows in your business journey. Your vision is now the guiding light that will steer every decision you make, ensuring alignment with your core values and long-term goals.

> **By clearly defining your personal and professional motivations, you've laid the foundation for everything that follows in your business journey.**

However, a vision without a plan remains just a dream. Now it's time to take that vision and turn it into an actionable strategy. In the next chapter, we'll move from vision to execution by organizing a clear, strategic path forward. This chapter will focus on how to create a road map that brings your vision to life—one step at a time—through intentional, structured planning. Let's dive into the practical steps needed to organize and strategize your way toward achieving the future you've envisioned.

# CHAPTER 8
# The Power of Organization

Once you've embraced the mindset of defining a clear vision for your business and begin auditing for gaps and opportunities, a new way of thinking takes over. This shift happens because having a well-defined vision changes how you approach every decision. It becomes difficult to operate without considering how each action moves you closer to your goals.

This mindset naturally extends into the realm of strategy. Just as vision defines your destination, strategy is the methodical process of getting there. The two are inseparable.

Strategy is a necessity. Without it, you are aimless, drifting without direction or purpose. You have no way to measure progress, no way to optimize your efforts, and no clear path forward. Strategy provides the structure and clarity needed to make informed decisions. It's not just about having a plan—it's about intentionally aligning every action to your long-term vision. Without strategy, even the best vision remains a distant wish. With it, you're equipped with the road map to turn that vision into a tangible reality. It's not enough to hope for success; strategy ensures you actively work toward it.

**Without strategy, even the best vision remains a distant wish.**

Strategy isn't limited to business. For instance, in personal finance, there's budgeting and financial management—strategically allocating income to manage expenses, save, and invest based on goals. In career development, you select skills to learn that align with market trends and personal aspirations to enhance employability. In sports, game plans leverage team strengths against opponent vulnerabilities, while player development focuses on individual skills that fit the team's needs. Even in education, curriculum design is strategic, balancing depth and breadth to prepare students effectively.

At its core, strategy is about making informed choices to achieve specific goals. Sometimes, the goal is to maintain and sustain—playing defense. Other times, it's about accelerating, seizing opportunities, or pivoting—playing offense. Strategy involves setting objectives and developing a plan to allocate resources and actions efficiently to achieve the objectives laid out in your vision. You've already defined the vision and set objectives through the audit. Now you'll develop the plan. Strategy is the how of pursuing and achieving the vision. It requires making thoughtful choices, considering what-ifs, and deciding not just what to do but also what *not* to do. These decisions are shaped by risk tolerance, intuition, and available resources. As we demonstrated in the SWOT analysis, strategy involves leveraging strengths while mitigating weaknesses in the face of external opportunities and threats.

Strategic formulation begins with clear goal-setting based on an organization's vision, establishing measurable and achievable objectives. Without strategy, your vision is just a wish. Strategy empowers the vision by grounding it in reality through planning and action. Knowing your vision makes goal-setting easier because you now have a direction—a North Star.

Next, you'll use thorough analysis—both of your internal capabilities and external market dynamics, competitive landscape, and economic conditions—to create a prioritized plan. Then, identify and evaluate various strategic options to determine which path aligns with your goals and best fits the anticipated environment. When you make decisions and take action, it's based on selecting the most suitable strategic option, considering all the factors that could impact that decision. Detailed action plans are then crafted, specifying responsibilities, resource allocation, and timelines. Once this strategic phase is complete, the execution phase involves implementing these plans through coordinated efforts, ensuring alignment with the identified objectives.

➤ **At its core, strategy is about making informed choices to achieve specific goals.**

No strategy is foolproof or guarantees success. Therefore, strategy must be dynamic, requiring ongoing monitoring and adaptation. It's almost inevitable that the moment you set a plan in place, something disrupts it. As the saying goes, "The best-laid plans of mice and men often go awry." This doesn't mean you should avoid planning; it highlights that strategy is always evolving. Unexpected challenges are part of the journey, and successful entrepreneurs recognize the importance of flexibility.

Having a dedicated strategist or even a strategic mindset is often necessary, especially during a pivot, because the mental exhaustion of consistently anticipating what comes next can be overwhelming. Accepting that things may not always go as planned normalizes the fact that even with the best of intentions and the most thorough plan, things still go wrong. And when they do, it's not necessarily a reflection of your circumstances or luck. Rather, it's a call to adjust, reassess, and keep moving forward with resilience.

> **By having a strategy, you can transform your weaknesses into strengths and your perceived disadvantages into powerful assets.**

Every story you've ever heard about an underdog beating the giant is because of strategy: the tortoise and the hare, David and Goliath, or even Rocky Balboa in the ring. In fact, many of the phrases we use from these tales are the actual strategies themselves: "Slow and steady wins the race" or "Divide and conquer." In each of those cases, the underdog was less resourced and seemingly destined to lose. Except, they had strategy, and they wielded it in a way that allowed them to come out victorious. By having a strategy, you can transform your weaknesses into strengths and your perceived disadvantages into powerful assets.

Strategy is about envisioning a future and systematically working toward it. It provides direction and focus, acting as a road map that outlines long-term goals and is also the means to achieve them. It aligns day-to-day operations with broader objectives, ensuring coherence and purpose in business activities.

## CONSEQUENCES OF SKIPPING STRATEGY

There are countless examples throughout history of businesses that failed due to poor strategic planning or an inability to adapt. One of the most notable is Kodak. Once a dominant force in the photography industry, Kodak revolutionized the market by making photography accessible to the masses. The founder's vision was simple: Make the camera as convenient as a pencil. Kodak achieved this in 1888 with the introduction of its first camera, which came preloaded with a hundred-exposure film roll. After customers used the roll, they would send the entire camera back to Kodak, where the film was developed, prints were made, and the camera was reloaded and returned. This innovative approach simplified the photographic process and made it user-friendly. The Brownie camera, introduced later and marketed toward children, further democratized photography with a one-dollar price tag, creating a mass market and cementing Kodak as a household name. The phrase "Kodak moment" became synonymous with capturing life's special memories.

Despite its success in film photography, Kodak was also a pioneer in digital technology. In 1975, one of Kodak's engineers invented the first digital camera. However, Kodak's leadership hesitated to pursue this groundbreaking innovation, fearing it would cannibalize their highly profitable film business. This reluctance to embrace the digital future marked the beginning of a series of strategic missteps.

As digital technology advanced in the 1990s and early 2000s, companies like Canon, Sony, and Nikon embraced the shift, leaving Kodak behind. Consumers eagerly adopted digital cameras, drawn to the convenience of digital storage and the elimination of film processing. By the time Kodak realized the importance of digital, it was too late. Although it eventually became one of the top sellers of digital cameras in the early 2000s, the profit margins were significantly lower than those from film. Kodak ventured into printers and other digital products, but these efforts failed to compensate for the rapid decline in film sales.

Once Kodak fully committed to the digital market, it was oversaturated, and the company struggled to maintain its competitive edge. In 2012, burdened by high costs, a bloated corporate structure, and a failure to adapt its business model in time, Kodak filed for Chapter 11 bankruptcy. Today, the company has restructured and focuses on niche markets, including imaging for businesses and motion picture film products. Kodak, once synonymous with personal photography, is no longer a dominant player in that space.

This story highlights the consequences of neglecting a forward-thinking strategy, particularly in the face of technological disruption and market evolution. While Kodak initially thrived as a leader in film photography, the company failed to align its strategy with the digital revolution. By clinging to its traditional film products, Kodak misallocated resources and allowed competitors to dominate the digital market.

Kodak's downfall serves as a cautionary tale, illustrating the importance of maintaining strategic foresight and adaptability. Success in the past doesn't guarantee future viability without a commitment to continual evaluation, innovation, and the flexibility to pivot when necessary. In today's rapidly evolving market, businesses must stay agile to ensure long-term relevance and competitiveness.

# THE ROLE OF STRATEGY IN SHAPING BUSINESS DECISIONS AND INFRASTRUCTURE

Every business decision contributes to the construction or modification of the business's infrastructure—its systems, processes, and organizational structure. While not every decision carries the same weight or becomes a cornerstone of this infrastructure, each one plays a part. Strategic planning provides the framework for these decisions, ensuring they align with long-term objectives and market conditions.

Think of construction: Imagine laying bricks without a clear design or plan, slathering mortar haphazardly and dropping bricks wherever it's convenient—some with care and others without. You might occasionally build a wall, pave a street, or create a pattern unintentionally, but there's no cohesive structure. That's what it looks like to approach business, projects, or life decisions without a clear strategy. Strategy prevents ad hoc decision-making that leads to inconsistencies and inefficiencies, often forcing you to pivot when things don't work out.

> ➤ **Strategy prevents ad hoc decision-making that leads to inconsistencies and inefficiencies.**

Conducting business this way often leads to resource shortages. Whether it's a lack of capital, human resources, or technology, if you're not considering the strain on different parts of your business, you'll eventually hit a constraint. Even worse, you might reach for a resource that you expect to have available—only to find it's gone.

One of our clients, a clinic owner, faced this issue. She had promoted one of her therapists to the role of clinical coordinator, relieving herself of many administrative duties. To fill the gap left by this promotion, another therapist was asked to take on additional responsibilities. However, friction arose with the second therapist, leading the clinic owner to consider terminating this individual. We discussed the various implications of this decision, such as the financial strain and the need to reassign the therapist's clients. While we suggested finding and training a replacement before proceeding with termination, the owner decided to immediately let go of the problematic therapist. As a result, the clinical coordinator had to take on the additional client load, and the administrative work returned to the owner.

Within weeks, the owner found herself overwhelmed by the administrative workload again. The clinical coordinator, who had already been assigned additional therapy work to cover the gap left by the fired therapist, became unhappy with the increased responsibilities. As a result, the clinic's culture and operations began to suffer. To compound the issue, a significant opportunity arose—one that, under normal circumstances, the clinic could have pursued. However, the strain caused by the sudden firing left them unable to seize it. What should have been a morale-boosting win turned into a missed opportunity. This single decision—a misplaced brick—impacted the clinic's trajectory for months. Eventually, the owner hired a replacement, and the situation improved, but the short-term strain had already taken its toll.

**However, strategic planning doesn't end with a one-time implementation; it fosters a culture of continuous improvement.**

Beyond resource allocation, strategic planning shines when applied to operational efficiency. This is an area we feel strongly about, as it's critical to scaling a business sustainably. Operations manage the day-to-day functions of a business, and efficiency ensures that those operations are optimized. Whether it's personnel, technology, or workflows, strategic planning plays a crucial role.

We have a mantra: "Automate, outsource, hire." This means that when solving workflow issues, the first step is to automate, often using technology. For instance, when someone signs up to become a customer through a website, using a tool like Zapier can automatically transfer their information to an email marketing platform, saving time and avoiding manual input. Once everything that can be automated has been addressed, the next step is outsourcing. Instead of hiring someone in-house, you can tap into external expertise when needed. This approach works best for project-based tasks, such as creating marketing materials. Finally, as a last resort, you might hire an employee to handle tasks that can't be automated or outsourced.

This approach increases operational efficiency because technology can scale indefinitely, handling tasks without the limitations of human capacity. Outsourcing ensures you stay in your zone of genius while delegating specialized work to experts in their fields. Only after maximizing these two options do you hire, keeping your business lean and efficient.

Operational efficiency is more than just managing your workforce effectively. Strategic planning plays a critical role in streamlining operations and eliminating redundancies. Whether it's optimizing your recruitment process to attract top talent quickly or reducing turnover through better onboarding practices, aligning your hiring strategy with operational goals can greatly enhance productivity and cost-effectiveness.

This may involve adopting lean principles, automating tasks, and reengineering processes for greater efficiency. The goal is to reduce waste—whether in time, resources, or effort—while improving output speed and quality.

However, strategic planning doesn't end with a one-time implementation; it fosters a culture of continuous improvement. Processes are regularly reviewed and updated, ensuring that each decision further strengthens your business's infrastructure.

That's the beauty of strategy—it's malleable. There are infinite ways to reach your goals, and strategy allows you the flexibility to adapt and refine your approach as you go but understanding the importance of strategy is only the beginning. Now, we need to dive deeper into how you can actively create and implement effective strategies. In the next chapter, we'll explore the essential components of building a strong strategic foundation, from gaining clarity and focus to ensuring alignment and developing actionable plans. This is where you move from concept to creation, turning your vision into an organized, structured path forward.

# CHAPTER 9
# The Power of Strategy

With a solid understanding of why strategy is crucial and how it can shape the future of your business, the next step is learning how to craft and implement it effectively.

Strategy isn't a one-size-fits-all solution; it's a dynamic process that requires clarity, focus, and alignment with your long-term goals. In this chapter, we'll dive into the practical side of creating a strategy—from knowing when to seek expert advice to building it step-by-step yourself. You'll learn how to develop clear action plans that keep you aligned with your vision and ensure that your business moves forward with purpose. This is where theory meets execution, guiding you in transforming strategic insights into tangible outcomes.

## WHEN TO SEEK EXPERT GUIDANCE

You may be wondering whether you possess the sophistication or knowledge to develop strategy on your own. Especially after seeing how crucial it is to your business, you might question whether you can do it effectively by yourself. You're also likely aware that strategist is an official profession, with experts dedicated to helping businesses strategize their growth and align with their visions. So, how can you assess whether your strategies are effective? Is it possible to do it yourself, or is this a case where professional assistance is essential?

➤ **This is where theory meets execution, guiding you in transforming strategic insights into tangible outcomes.**

The answer to whether you can handle strategy independently depends on the complexity of your situation. There's no one-size-fits-all approach for any business or individual. Do you have business partners? Is there financial risk or debt involved in your decisions? How might others be affected by the pivot you're considering? For instance, a business launching a new offering validated by its audience and requiring minimal resources might proceed with limited planning. However, a business contemplating discontinuing an offering with potential layoffs or a shift in clientele could greatly benefit from in-depth strategic planning or professional advisory.

Your level of confidence in handling strategic tasks yourself also plays a part. If you doubt your objectivity in decision making or worry about holding yourself accountable, outside help might be wise. On the other hand, if you've pivoted successfully before and feel confident in your ability to continue, you might be fine doing it yourself for now.

Often, working with a strategist provides significant value. A successful strategy requires perspective, and as a business owner, you might be too close to your work to see the big picture. This proximity can lead to missed opportunities or overlooked problems. Having someone with an external viewpoint can reveal fresh insights and challenge assumptions. After all, it's hard to see the full landscape when you're standing in the middle of the picture.

Even as professional strategists, we use strategists for our own business. It's always easier to spot issues and opportunities in someone else's business than in your own. Strategists offer this vital external perspective, helping you see things you might otherwise miss, especially when significant decisions are at stake.

Affordability is often a concern when considering hiring a strategist, but resource constraints don't necessarily mean you can't get valuable strategic insight. You can create informal opportunities for strategic consultation by gathering trusted friends, colleagues, or mentors for discussions. These low-cost strategy sessions can yield meaningful feedback and help refine your plans.

The need for a strategist grows, however, as the complexity and risk of your decisions increase. If your decision could have far-reaching consequences or involves significant risks, the expertise of a strategist becomes not just helpful but essential. Their insights help prevent missteps and maximize the potential for success.

A strategist's role isn't just to avoid failure—they also help unlock opportunities. Whether it's expanding your market share or increasing capacity, a strategist can guide you in evaluating offers carefully and seizing opportunities strategically.

→ **Strategists don't just help you avoid pitfalls— they guide you toward meaningful opportunities and long-term success.**

In some cases, strategists also engage in scenario planning, helping you map out multiple pathways to success. By anticipating various future outcomes, you can make more informed decisions, preparing for both expected and unexpected developments. Their knowledge of industry trends and competitive dynamics also ensures that you stay ahead, positioning your business to lead, innovate, and thrive.

In short, strategists don't just help you avoid pitfalls—they guide you toward meaningful opportunities and long-term success. Whether you hire a professional or rely on informal strategy discussions, the insights you gain can help you make well-informed decisions that align with your goals and minimize risks.

## HOW TO CREATE STRATEGY

You'll be glad to know that much of the hard work in creating a strategy for yourself and your business is already done. You've already committed to making the necessary personal and emotional changes to move forward, conducted an audit, identified your priorities, and articulated your vision. As a result, the remaining steps are simple. These steps include creating clear objectives, developing timelines or priorities around those objectives, and detailing the necessary actions for execution. This strategic process does more than just push you toward your goals; it also builds a dynamic framework designed to help you remain resilient and responsive to internal changes and market conditions as you adapt and evolve over time.

Regularly revisiting your emotional and personal develop-ment, conducting audits to extract actionable information, and refining your vision to align with new goals is part of a simple and repeatable process. The beauty of repeatable processes in business, especially as you scale, lies in the consistency they create. The PIVOT framework becomes your go-to solution for determining next steps, address-ing internal questions, and crafting an actionable plan. It's about more than just pivoting; it's about maintaining stra-tegic alignment with where you want to go. Since there are infinite ways to execute, your strategy should become a living process that evolves with your needs and responds to shifts in the market.

## 1. Set Objective Goals

Strategizing is about thinking critically and creatively to achieve your desired outcomes. The first step is setting clear, objective, and measurable goals. Assuming you've already conducted an audit, these goals should be evident. Each goal should support the broader vision you've identified for your-self and be specific enough to allow you to measure progress. This is where we start reverse engineering your desires into small, actionable steps. We begin with the end in mind—your ultimate vision—and work backward to map out the steps required to get from your current position to that goal.

However, one key exception is if your audit revealed an imme-diate compliance issue. Areas related to legal, finance, taxes, entity status, trademarking, or any other compliance matter must be addressed as a priority. While strategic planning will still be necessary to allocate the appropriate resources to resolve these concerns, compliance must take precedence over other business objectives. Once these critical issues are resolved, you can refocus on aligning your goals with the broader vision of your business.

Once any immediate compliance concerns are addressed, we can refocus on aligning your objectives with your long-term vision. For instance, if your vision is financial freedom, we would first define what that looks like for you. From there, we'd trace the milestones leading to that outcome. Perhaps one milestone is increasing your revenue by 20 percent within the next twenty-four months. This would then break down further into smaller, manageable objectives, such as launching a new product line or entering three new markets by year's end. Working backward from your vision allows you to chart a path that is both realistic and aligned with your goals.

As you develop your objectives, it's essential to leverage the insights gained from your SWOT analysis. You now have a clear understanding of your strengths and opportunities, as well as the weaknesses and threats that could hinder

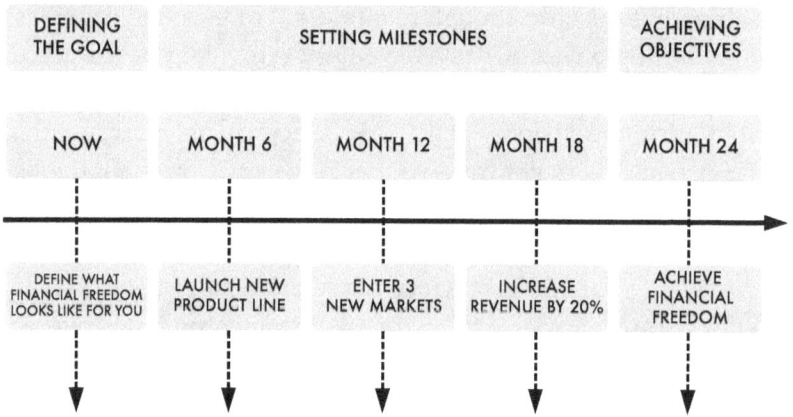

## STEPS TO FINANCIAL FREEDOM

| DEFINING THE GOAL | SETTING MILESTONES | | | ACHIEVING OBJECTIVES |
| --- | --- | --- | --- | --- |
| NOW | MONTH 6 | MONTH 12 | MONTH 18 | MONTH 24 |
| DEFINE WHAT FINANCIAL FREEDOM LOOKS LIKE FOR YOU | LAUNCH NEW PRODUCT LINE | ENTER 3 NEW MARKETS | INCREASE REVENUE BY 20% | ACHIEVE FINANCIAL FREEDOM |

your progress. The next step is to turn that knowledge into an actionable strategy. Align your objectives with your strengths and the opportunities they offer. For instance, one of our clients recognized that her team's clinical expertise was a key differentiator in a competitive market. To capitalize on this strength, we helped her emphasize her team's credentials and innovative approaches in their marketing efforts, successfully setting her business apart.

## Formulating a strategy involves determining the best course of action to achieve your goals.

However, strengths and opportunities are only part of the equation. It's equally important to address your weaknesses and mitigate threats. Another client faced a recurring issue with high turnover in a key sales role. Since it was an entry-level position, turnover was inevitable. Instead of fighting the reality, we adapted by restructuring the organization, creating detailed SOPs, and redefining responsibilities. This approach ensured that when turnover occurred, the business remained stable and operations continued smoothly.

Formulating a strategy involves determining the best course of action to achieve your goals. It's about deciding *how* to reach the objectives you've set, considering both your internal capabilities and external opportunities. Start by linking strategies to your objectives. If one objective is to increase market share by 20 percent within two years, a strategy could involve diversifying offerings or intensifying marketing in key areas. There are multiple ways to achieve an objective, so brainstorm several options. Evaluate each based on feasibility, risk, impact, and how well they align with your available resources. You don't have to do this alone—resources like brainstorming sessions, online research, networking, and even tools like ChatGPT can all be valuable.

## 2. Develop Tactics

Once the objectives are defined, the next step is to develop tactics—the actionable steps that will help you achieve each objective. Tactics should be designed to leverage your strengths, address weaknesses, capitalize on opportunities, and mitigate threats. They need to be specific, realistic, and directly tied to your goals to ensure measurable progress.

When crafting tactics, start by examining your strengths: How can you use them to seize opportunities or counter-act threats? Next, address your weaknesses: What specific actions can you take to minimize their impact or improve upon them? Then, focus on maximizing opportunities: What initiatives can help you take full advantage of favorable external factors? Finally, consider threats: What proactive steps can you implement to reduce their impact?

### ➤ Tactics should be designed to leverage your strengths, address weaknesses, capitalize on opportunities, and mitigate threats.

Returning to the example of capturing 20 percent more market share in the next twelve months, you might start by leveraging an existing strength—like a strong digital marketing team—by launching targeted social media campaigns aimed at reaching a new demographic. If a weakness, such as a lack of data analytics expertise, is identified, you might hire or train staff to improve the team's ability to understand and engage with this new audience.

Opportunities should also be fully explored. For instance, partnering with industry influencers who already have credibility with your target market can significantly boost visibility and engagement. At the same time, it's important to account for potential threats—such as increased competition from larger brands. Having a contingency plan to counter these pressures will help protect your market position and support sustained growth.

Once you've generated a range of options, assess each one by considering factors like expected benefits, costs, and resource needs. Tools like cost-benefit analysis, risk assessment, or ROI projections can provide valuable insights, many of which are readily accessible online. If this step feels overly complex, it might be a sign that your strategy requires outside expertise, in which case outsourcing could be a viable option. Ultimately, after evaluating your options, prioritize the strategies that offer the highest impact and best align with your resources and capabilities.

### 3. Assign Tasks

With clear tactics in place, the next step is to break them down into actionable tasks and assign ownership to individuals or teams. This ensures accountability and steady progress. Each task should have a specific deadline and measurable outcome, allowing for effective tracking and adjustments along the way.

To assign tasks effectively, begin by breaking each tactic into manageable steps. Identify which tasks can be delegated to external professionals or handled internally by team members. When outsourcing, be clear about deliverables, deadlines, and expectations, ensuring the external party understands how their work aligns with your overall strategy. For internal tasks, focus on matching team members with responsibilities that play to their strengths and capacity. Setting clear deadlines and scheduling regular check-ins will help maintain accountability and keep progress on track.

→ **To assign tasks effectively, begin by breaking each tactic into manageable steps.**

For example, if your objective is to increase market share by 10 percent in a new demographic, the tasks might include outsourcing demographic research to a marketing consultant or freelance researcher, who would be responsible for delivering detailed audience personas. Next, you could assign the creation of targeted ad content to a freelance content creator or digital marketing expert familiar with the platforms where your target demographic is most active. A digital marketer could then be tasked with setting up and managing social media ads, optimizing their performance as the campaign progresses.

Additionally, you might contract a freelance analyst to set up and monitor analytics tools to track engagement and conversions, providing regular reports on campaign performance for data-driven adjustments. You could personally handle researching potential partnerships with influencers or delegate this task to a virtual assistant who initiates influencer outreach and reports back on opportunities. By outsourcing or assigning these tasks to the right professionals, you ensure that every aspect of your strategy is executed efficiently, even if you're operating with a small in-house team.

## CLARITY

A good strategy is articulated so that it leaves no ambiguity about what needs to be achieved. Clarity in strategy means the objectives, the means to achieve them, and the roles and responsibilities of everyone involved are explicitly stated.

For example, imagine a small business with the objective

of launching a new product within six months. The strategy might include clear, measurable steps, such as product development, market testing, and marketing rollout. Each of these steps would have defined ownership: the product team is responsible for development, the marketing team handles testing and promotion, and the operations team manages inventory and distribution. Additionally, timelines and milestones are established for each phase. This ensures that every team knows exactly what their responsibilities are, the deadlines they must meet, and how their work contributes to the overall goal of launching the product on time. No one is left guessing what their role is or how success will be measured.

This clarity helps prevent misunderstandings and ensures there is a common understanding of the direction and priorities when it comes to what happens next. More than that, it creates ownership. There is no ambiguity in who has ownership of what tasks, projects, or outcomes. This also prevents misunderstandings and miscommunication because when a project or task lacks a clearly defined owner, the possibility of things not getting done is high. One of the beauties of having clarity is that it simplifies decision-making processes and reduces complexity in executing tasks, as each step and its purpose are clearly defined. Taking the time to spell all of this out in the beginning reduces the number of decisions that have to be made later, which cuts down on decision fatigue and reduces the chances for errors and oversight.

## FOCUS

Focus in strategy refers to the concentration of resources and efforts on key areas that will have the most significant impact on achieving your goals. A focused strategy does not try to address all problems or capitalize on every opportunity; instead, it prioritizes actions based on their potential to drive the most meaningful outcomes.

Take, for instance, a business that is launching a new service and has identified three areas for growth: expanding its customer base, developing a new product line, and optimizing current operational efficiency. Instead of trying to tackle all three simultaneously, a focused strategy might involve dedicating the next six months solely to expanding the customer base. This could include targeted marketing campaigns, customer outreach, and partnerships to grow the client pool. By concentrating on customer acquisition first, the business can build a stronger foundation before exploring product development or improving operations, ensuring that resources aren't spread too thin and momentum isn't lost.

This prioritization is crucial in a world of limited resources, where trying to do too much can dilute efforts and lead to suboptimal results. A lack of focus will subvert more of your plans than risk ever will. In order to build momentum, you need concentrated efforts. Diluting those efforts with a diffused focus on too many obstacles or opportunities will prevent you from achieving what you want. Focus helps in maintaining the discipline necessary to channel resources and energy into pursuits that matter most to your success.

## ALIGNMENT

Alignment ensures that the strategy is in harmony with your overarching vision and values, as well as its current resources and capabilities. If this book is about nothing else, it's about alignment—or getting back into a place with yourself and your business where you feel comfortable and compelled to take on the next thing. Strategic goals should reflect your long-term vision and consider what is realistically achievable given your internal strengths and weaknesses and the external opportunities and threats.

Consider a small business whose vision is to scale while maintaining a high level of customer service. The business may be tempted to implement aggressive growth strategies, such as expanding into new markets or acquiring other businesses. However, if customer service is a core value and there are already signs that the current team is stretched thin, these expansion efforts could compromise that value. A strategy that aligns with both the growth vision and the company's commitment to customer service would involve first addressing internal capacity—hiring and training more staff or optimizing operations—before pursuing aggressive expansion. This ensures that the business remains true to its values while pursuing growth in a way that is sustainable and manageable.

If you're a larger organization, a good strategy aligns the objectives of various departments and teams, ensuring their efforts are complementary and synergistic rather than conflicting or redundant. The same applies when you build out a strategy for your life, your family, or your business. You need enough overlap to ensure that momentum from one area benefits the other but not so much redundancy that it diminishes efforts. This consistency is essential for smooth operations (in business and life) and helps build cohesion in which all components work toward a unified goal.

A strategy that embodies clarity, focus, and alignment is more likely to be effective because it guides the organization with precision, directs resources judiciously, and ensures cohesive efforts across all levels. This leads to better performance outcomes, higher efficiency, and greater adaptability to changing circumstances. Such a strategy also facilitates better communication internally and externally, enhancing collaboration and support for strategic initiatives. Ultimately, the goodness of a strategy is measured by its ability to facilitate decision-making that reliably moves you toward your desired state in a manageable, sustainable, and predictable manner while being robust enough to adapt as conditions change.

## DETAILED ACTION PLANS

The final step in strategy creation is converting strategies into detailed action plans. This crucial step involves transforming high-level strategies into tangible, executable tasks. Each action plan should clearly outline what actions need to be taken, by whom, with what resources, and by when. It's important to meticulously specify each component to ensure clarity and accountability.

To start, define the specific actions required to achieve each strategy. Break these down into individual tasks and, most importantly, assign ownership. As mentioned earlier, only one person should be the owner of a task or project and be responsible for its completion, even if aspects of the task are outsourced. This person manages and oversees the process from start to finish, ensuring accountability and preventing tasks from slipping through the cracks. Each individual assigned must also have the authority and capability to execute their responsibilities effectively.

Establishing clear deadlines for each action is equally critical. Realistic timelines create a sense of urgency and allow for efficient monitoring of progress. These deadlines should account for other ongoing activities in your business or personal life, providing a manageable balance.

To keep everything organized, you can break these strategies down into individual projects, group them into separate initiatives, or track them as KPIs across departments or personnel.

1. **Project Management:** Break down large-scale strategies into manageable projects. Each project should have a clearly defined scope, budget, team, and milestones. This format helps manage the workload more effectively, allowing for focused attention on complex tasks.
2. **Separate Initiatives:** For broader strategic goals, group actions into initiatives. For example, actions related to digital transformation could all fall under a single initiative. This structure creates synergy among related tasks and streamlines both management and reporting.
3. **KPIs (Key Performance Indicators):** Use KPIs to measure the success and effectiveness of these initiatives. While we'll dive deeper into KPIs in the next chapter, they provide measurable benchmarks to gauge progress and results.

This detailed approach ensures that your strategic goals are not only met but that your business develops a culture of accountability, precision, and adaptability. Keep in mind that this is just another iteration of the million different hows when it comes to accomplishing these action plans. Each task, deadline, and responsible person becomes a critical cog in the larger machine of strategic execution, driving you toward your goals.

Here is an example of what this might look like:

| SWOT Element | Objective | Tactic | Assigned Task | Timeline | KPI |
|---|---|---|---|---|---|
| **Strength:** Strong leadership and visionary owner<br><br>**Weakness:** High employee turnover<br><br>**Opportunity:** Increased availability of talent due to industry layoffs<br><br>**Threat:** Negative impact on team morale and productivity | Reduce employee turnover by 15 percent over the next 12 months while improving team morale. | 1. Conduct employee satisfaction surveys to identify retention issues.<br>2. Develop an employee engagement program.<br>3. Implement a mentorship program to support new hires. | Manager to conduct surveys and analyze results by Month 1.<br><br>Owner, manager, and lead associate to design an engagement program by Month 3.<br><br>Managers to facilitate mentorship meetings by Month 4. | Month 1: Conduct surveys.<br><br>Months 2–3: Develop engagement program.<br><br>Month 4: Launch mentorship program.<br><br>Month 6: Evaluate results. | 1. Percentage decrease in turnover rate.<br><br>2. Employee satisfaction score improvement.<br><br>3. Participation rate in mentorship program. |

# THE ROLE OF STRATEGY MOVING FORWARD

Implementing a deliberate and methodical strategic planning process helps avoid the pitfalls of sloppy decision-making and reverting to outdated habits. It's common to drift back into familiar patterns that may no longer align with the business's current needs or ambitions. Developing the discipline to prioritize strategy as the go-to approach takes time, but with practice, it becomes second nature. The integration of vision and strategy is crucial in this process. Even if the strategy begins to lose momentum, keeping your vision front and center ensures that the objectives you've set to work toward that vision remain relevant and guiding.

Adopting a slow, steady pace when implementing new strategies is essential. Rushing through changes can result in oversights and errors, making it easier to fall back into old habits. By taking the time to thoroughly understand and integrate new processes, you set the stage for long-term success. This gradual approach also allows for refining strategies over time, incorporating feedback, and adjusting based on real-world results.

➤ **Implementing a deliberate and methodical strategic planning process helps avoid the pitfalls of sloppy decision-making and reverting to outdated habits.**

Consistency across all strategies is key. Although we discuss strategy in individual formats, none of this work happens in isolation. Business continues as you implement strategic pivots, and rarely do we get the luxury of pausing everything to transform fully. It's far messier than that. Ensuring that all strategies align and reinforce one another is critical to building momentum. This also extends to stakeholders: unanimous buy-in is vital. You can't afford for any department, partner, or investor to make decisions that deviate from your strategic direction. Cohesive strategies keep all efforts moving in the same direction, increasing efficiency and the likelihood of success. This coherence simplifies oversight and minimizes confusion among those involved.

Finally, strategic planning is not a one-time event but a continuous process. Regularly reviewing your strategies and their outcomes is essential for ensuring their effectiveness. These reviews help assess whether the strategy is working as intended or if inefficiencies are creeping back in.

## TURNING STRATEGY INTO ACTION

Transitioning from the meticulous work of strategy development to the dynamic process of implementation marks a critical shift in turning vision into reality. Up to this point, we've focused on how to craft a clear, focused, and aligned strategy that is both actionable and adaptable. You've laid the groundwork by creating detailed plans and ensuring that every aspect of your strategy supports your overarching goals.

Now it's time to move from planning to action.

The true test of a strategy lies not in its formulation but in its execution. A well-crafted strategy is only as good as the actions that bring it to life. The next phase, *transformation*, is about taking those carefully designed plans and putting them into motion. This is where your vision begins to materialize, where the abstract becomes tangible, and where your business starts to evolve in real time.

**A well-crafted strategy is only as good as the actions that bring it to life.**

In the next chapter, we'll explore the nuances of implementation—how to effectively execute your strategy, overcome challenges, and ensure that every effort contributes to your long-term goals. Execution requires discipline, adaptability, and a relentless focus on results. It's where your leadership, decision-making, and team alignment will be tested and proven. The strategies you've developed are your road map, but this chapter is about driving the vehicle, navigating obstacles, and staying the course until you reach your destination.

As we step into transformation, we'll discuss the tools, mindsets, and practices essential for successful execution. This is where strategy meets reality and where your commitment to your vision will be truly realized.

# CHAPTER 10

# The Power of Transformation

With your strategy in place, you now enter the implementation phase, where transformation begins to take shape. Transformation, especially in the context of executing new strategies and leading a business, is not a one-time event but an ongoing, evolving process. It requires consistent development, adjustment, and refinement over time. Implementation rarely occurs in a straight line—there will be moments of progress followed by periods of recalibration or setbacks. While you can create plans that account for various variables, the reality is that things often deviate from those plans. This unpredictability is part of working with complex systems and navigating the ever-changing dynamics of business.

Therefore, flexibility and adaptability become essential in guiding you through this phase. Transformation is not simply about achieving a final goal; it's about continually evolving and adapting both as an individual and as an organization. The true value lies in who you become through the process, not just the destination you reach. This chapter will guide you through how to implement your strategy effectively while embracing the ongoing, dynamic nature of transformation.

## THE JOURNEY TO JOY THROUGH STRATEGIC SUCCESS

The early stages of implementing new strategies can feel daunting, as they often require significant shifts in both mindset and operations. If you've been accustomed to playing defense in business, transitioning to a more proactive, offensive position will take some adjustment. However, overcoming these initial hurdles is about more than just weathering tough times—it's about laying the groundwork for future success. As your strategies begin to take shape and early signs of progress emerge, there's a profound sense of accomplishment can reignite the passion that originally inspired you to start your business.

**Transformation is not a one-time event but an ongoing, evolving process.**

One of the most exhilarating aspects of being a business owner is watching your vision turn into reality. This phase of strategy implementation is particularly rewarding as the tangible outcomes of strategic decisions—whether hitting sales targets, entering new markets, or receiving positive customer feedback—begin to surface. The joy of seeing your ideas work effectively in the real world validates the risks you've taken and reinforces your commitment to your business goals.

> **The true value lies in who you become through the process, not just the destination you reach.**

There's immense satisfaction in solving problems, innovating solutions, and pushing past limitations, especially when you've done the inner work of reshaping beliefs and core values. Implementing business strategies often involves facing numerous challenges—perceived or real, internal or external. Each challenge overcome becomes a building block for personal and professional growth. You're never the same person afterward; you never go back to zero, even if, on paper, you appear to be starting over. You now carry the practice, wisdom, and confidence you didn't have before. These victories are not only business achievements but personal triumphs that renew your sense of purpose and excitement in your work.

It's important not only to acknowledge your efforts but also to celebrate your milestones and achievements along the way. These celebrations mark your progress and provide opportunities to reflect on how far you've come. This isn't solely about outcomes; it's about recognizing how you show up and who you're becoming.

We had a client who joined us for an immersive session to revamp her service offerings. When we started, we realized she had drifted away from her true passion. Known for her strategic visual design work for Etsy stores and physical product shops, she had allowed herself to be molded into a social media graphic creator in response to market demands. She had lost sight of her vision. The first thing we did was guide her back to that vision. We scrapped her current service offerings and rebuilt her business strategy from the ground up. Although it would take months before the new services launched, in that single session, she transformed. She rediscovered her passion, reconnected with her expertise, and regained her confidence. That shift—her renewed conviction in herself—was a milestone worth celebrating. It wasn't about money or follower counts; it was about an internal shift that would eventually lead to external success.

As strategies unfold and objectives are met, take time to reflect on the personal growth experienced along the way. Every decision made, problem solved, and adaptation to change is a lesson in business and life. How you approach one thing is often how you approach everything. As you begin creating a vision for your business, you'll find yourself applying those same principles in your relationships, lifestyle choices, and beyond. This work is not confined to business; it permeates all aspects of your life. You'll find yourself being strategic in how you plan vacations, purchase a car, or fit workouts into your schedule. When you have a clear framework to guide you—1) prepare by assessing your emotions and readiness, 2) audit your current circumstances, 3) set your vision, 4) create a plan, and 5) execute with intention—there are truly no limits to how you can transform and apply these steps to achieve your goals. This continuous learning and application of knowledge is a critical component of finding joy in business and life. It transforms routine work into a dynamic journey of personal and professional growth, offering continuous opportunities to advance and apply what you've learned.

**→ How you approach one thing is often how you approach everything.**

Rediscovering joy in business through the strategic execution of your vision means connecting day-to-day actions to larger goals, celebrating small wins and major milestones, and growing both as a leader and an individual. This renewed passion is not just fundamental for personal fulfillment but also for the sustainable success of your business. Once you start building your business and life this way, you won't want to do it any other way—we're living proof of that. We believe in it so strongly, we wrote an entire book about it!

## BUILDING RESILIENCE

In the business world, resilience refers to the ability to withstand disruptions, adapt to changes, and continue pursuing objectives effectively. It's not merely about survival but about evolving in response to challenges and emerging stronger. While resilience is sometimes called grit when operating defensively, a more proactive approach to business is where resilience truly shines. Resilience here means the ability to navigate back and forth between defensive reactions to challenges and proactive efforts to continue your journey. This adaptability is a critical factor in sustaining long-term success, as it encompasses both managing immediate crises and preparing for future ones. In fact, resilience is the essence of bouncing back and forth between these dynamics. Increasing your resilience is one of the key transformations you'll experience by applying the principles from this book.

The first step in improving your bounce-back rate is to cultivate a resilient mindset. This means viewing challenges not as insurmountable obstacles but as opportunities to learn and grow. As we outlined as one of our takeaways in the introduction, there are no losses—only lessons to grow from. Resilience, then, is about finding the lesson in the challenge, not assuming failure. A resilient mindset is characterized by optimism and a willingness to experiment and take calculated risks. As you've learned, optimism is a choice, calculated risk is tied to strategy, and experimentation is essential for achieving your vision. Optimism enables you to see difficulties as temporary and surmountable, helping you maintain motivation even in tough times. Meanwhile, a resilient mindset embraces stepping out of your comfort zone and trying new approaches—qualities that will carry you forward in any challenge.

→ **A resilient mindset is characterized by optimism and a willingness to experiment and take calculated risks.**

Building resilience through strategic planning shifts you from a reactive stance, merely responding to external events, to a proactive one in which you shape and influence future outcomes. Being proactive makes you more agile. With plans in place for various possibilities, you can pivot quickly without the paralysis that often accompanies unforeseen challenges. This means you've identified potential risks early, assessed their likelihood and impact, and implemented strategies to mitigate them. By avoiding crisis mode—often associated with hurried, expensive decisions—you operate more efficiently and reduce costs associated with unexpected events.

Just as the human nervous system processes and responds to stimuli, a business has its own organizational nervous system composed of communication channels, decision-making processes, and feedback loops. This system helps sense external changes—market trends, competition, and technological advancements—and translate them into strategic actions. Developing this organizational nervous system is like building a muscle—it takes practice. The more reps you give yourself, the quicker your learning will be and the faster your business will respond to challenges.

The first step is becoming more sensitive to the signals your business is receiving. In biological terms, enhancing sensory capabilities involves improving the sensitivity of receptors to detect stimuli. In business, this translates to improving how you gather and analyze data. You must tune your spidey senses to detect challenges and opportunities before they fully materialize. With one of our clients, for instance, we used monthly KPIs to track how close her multiple studios were to hitting their sales goals. Seeing that data regularly allows us to identify challenges before the quarter ends.

Once data is processed, the nervous system needs quick decision-making to generate timely responses. Similarly, businesses need efficient decision-making processes to reduce delays, which is where strategic planning becomes crucial. For that same client, we developed contingency plans for each studio if it fell short of its sales goals, ensuring we wouldn't be scrambling at the last minute. Just as the nervous system coordinates responses with muscles and organs, businesses need alignment between strategy, people, and operational processes. All the sales managers and associates understood the plan, bought into it, and recognized the consequences of not meeting their targets.

> **Every challenge provides valuable data that can help refine your strategy and operations.**

Learning and memory in the nervous system strengthen effective neural pathways. In business, this translates into institutionalizing successful strategies and processes. That's how we developed the sales strategy—drawing on past experiences to craft a solution that works. Neuroplasticity, or the nervous system's ability to adapt to changes, is key to long-term health. Likewise, businesses need to remain flexible and adaptable to evolve with changing circumstances—a skill you'll develop through implementing this book's strategies. Look at that—not only are we solving your business challenges, but we're also helping you build a healthier, more adaptable approach.

Every challenge provides valuable data that can help refine your strategy and operations. You may achieve mastery in one area of your business—such as operational efficiency—only to find that the next challenge arises in leadership development. The more you learn from past experiences, the quicker you'll respond to future challenges. Each challenge you face strengthens your resilience and reduces downtime, allowing you to bounce back faster and with greater confidence.

## MEASURING RESILIENCE

Developing resilience is a multifaceted endeavor that enhances your agility and robustness, positioning you to capitalize on challenges and transform potential threats into opportunities. Measuring the success of resilience in a business context is crucial for understanding how effectively you can anticipate, respond to, and recover from challenges. Establishing clear metrics and indicators helps you gauge your resilience and refine strategies accordingly.

At the heart of business resilience is adaptability—the ability to quickly and effectively adjust to new conditions, disruptions, or unexpected challenges. Adaptability is not just about coping during a crisis; it's about continuously evolving your business practices to stay ahead of potential disruptions. This brings us to preparedness, another critical component of resilience. Preparation involves not only planning for what is expected but also developing comprehensive risk management and scenario planning for the unexpected. Successful preparation includes understanding potential risks, evaluating their impact, and creating strategic responses. Measuring success here involves reviewing how these plans are executed during crises and how they contribute to business continuity. For instance, how much did you rely on your contingency plans? Were they robust enough? If not, you'll need to further develop them for future reliance.

If reading all of this feels overwhelming, that's completely understandable—your resilience and adaptability may not be fully developed yet. You just need more reps.

While finalizing this book, we had a major ten-day trip planned to Italy, leaving our two young daughters at home with our moms. At the last minute, two completely unexpected events occurred, forcing us to change plans. One adjustment turned into another, and yet another.

**Resilience is a skill honed over time, and developing it requires intentionality and practice.**

Even after multiple iterations, the ultimate solution was to cut our trip short by a day and return home earlier than planned. Normally, a situation like this might send someone into a tailspin. This was a trip we had been planning for nearly a year, with flights and hotels booked months in advance. But none of that mattered when the unexpected happened.

All the preparation in the world couldn't account for these events. So, we adapted—almost unfazed—because we've put in the reps. After more than a decade of building resilience to unforeseen challenges in both our business and personal lives, adapting to sudden changes is almost second nature.

Resilience is a skill honed over time, and developing it

requires intentionality and practice. But how can you objectively measure resilience in your business? That's where data comes into play.

Shifting to a more objective approach, key performance indicators (KPIs) are essential metrics used to quantitatively assess the effectiveness and success of various business activities. They provide a clear, objective way to evaluate performance, offering data-driven insights into how well different areas of the business are functioning. KPIs are instrumental in monitoring the success of resilience strategies, as they allow you to track performance over time and see how well you're managing risks and recovering from disruptions. By helping you set goals and identify benchmarks, KPIs provide a mechanism for feedback on progress toward those goals. Most importantly, they ensure that day-to-day operations are aligned with broader strategic objectives. KPIs should be directly tied to your strategic initiatives and can measure anything that is objective—whether it's the number of emails sent to meet sales goals, monthly profits to monitor cash flow, or turnover rates to track customer retention. By working backward from your goals, you can define specific KPIs that ensure you're strategically moving in the right direction.

When it comes to resilience, there are three key KPIs to focus on: time to recover, financial stability, and operational performance.

1. **Time to Recover (TTR)** measures how long it takes for operations to return to normal performance levels after a disruption. A shorter TTR indicates greater agility and resilience, minimizing downtime and costs. To track TTR, first define what "normal performance" looks like for your operations. Then, after a disruption, measure the time from the disruption's onset until full

functionality is restored—or, if you pivot, how long it takes to implement the new course of action.

2. **Financial Stability Indicators** measure economic resilience, using metrics like cash flow and profitability to assess how well your business can withstand financial shocks while maintaining operations.

3. **Operational Performance Metrics** evaluate how well your systems and processes function under various conditions. High performance in these areas signals that your operations are resilient enough to adapt when challenges arise, whether internal or external.

While these KPIs are important, they aren't always necessary to track if your business primarily stays in an offensive position. If you're vigilant about your regular KPIs and start noticing dips early, you'll have the ability to respond before you even need to measure resilience. Take our client with multiple studios, for example. By tracking monthly KPIs, she avoids any surprises in quarterly reports, allowing her to make small adjustments along the way rather than scrambling to address larger issues down the road.

It's also essential to account for seasonality, particularly for retail or physical locations. Understanding what is normal for your industry during different times of the year will help you differentiate between expected fluctuations and genuine problems.

Beyond KPIs, accountability is crucial to ensure resilience strategies are effectively executed. This means clearly defining roles and responsibilities. For each goal, there should be one designated owner for each goal who's responsible for its outcome. Clarity in these roles ensures that everyone knows their part in contributing to the overall objective. These roles should be tied to specific KPIs, and regular check-ins, updates, and audits will help monitor progress and ensure accountability. This was illustrated in the table we provided in Chapter 9. When KPIs or objectives aren't being met, feedback loops allow for course correction, whether that involves adjusting strategies or imposing consequences. Feedback loops are created through regular reviews, performance tracking, and open communication. This might include weekly check-ins, data analysis, or quarterly assessments to ensure that issues are identified early and necessary adjustments are made. Effective feedback loops ensure accountability leads to continuous improvement rather than just punitive action.

For example, our client's sales manager checks the data weekly and makes adjustments with sales associates as needed. The owner reviews the data monthly and adjusts with the sales manager as necessary. Critical metrics like lead generation, conversion rates, or merchandise sales are placed on the weekly meeting agenda to ensure they are monitored closely.

In summary, evaluating the success of resilience in your business requires a comprehensive approach that integrates adaptability, KPIs, and accountability mechanisms. Adaptability ensures swift responses to changes, maintaining business continuity and competitiveness. KPIs provide objective measures of performance in areas such as recovery time, financial stability, and operational efficiency. Accountability ensures that everyone is responsible for executing resilience strategies and achieving their outcomes. Together, these elements form a robust framework for assessing resilience, helping you not only withstand challenges but also emerge stronger and better prepared for future adversities.

While quantitative measures like KPIs are critical, don't forget about qualitative assessments such as customer feedback, employee satisfaction surveys, or even your own sense of accomplishment and well-being. These softer metrics provide valuable insights into your progress and the overall health of your business.

## CONTINUOUS PRACTICE AND APPLICATION

As already suggested, we become inherently strategic thinkers and develop neural pathways to ensure we have a proactive mindset through continuous practice. As Malcolm Gladwell famously states in *Outliers*, it takes ten thousand hours of focused practice to achieve mastery in any field.[14] When considering a skill set like pivoting seamlessly and incorporating strategic planning into every aspect of your business and life, it will take years of practice. This isn't meant to discourage you but rather to remind you to give yourself grace.

➤ **The best way to build this capability is through what we call messy action.**

Developing this skill takes time and effort. The best way to build this capability is through what we call messy action. In a more formal sense, this means taking iterative action on your ideas and goals while applying what you learn along the way. In fact, this iterative approach is often more advanced and efficient for making necessary changes in a business and learning about yourself, as it forces continuous reflection. This process involves not just acquiring knowledge but applying it in real-world scenarios and refining your approach based on feedback.

[14]Gladwell, Malcolm. 2011. Outliers: The Story of Success. New York: Little, Brown.

This method closely resembles *quality improvement* models, which consist of regularly alternating between planning, doing, studying, and acting. Growth begins with the acquisition of new knowledge—whether through formal education, self-directed learning, or new experiences. The next step is applying this knowledge in practical settings. This is why we advocate for messy action and launching with a minimally viable offer. The idea is to put theory into practice in a controlled, manageable way before committing to full-scale implementation. If you start on a small scale, where risks are manageable, and you can learn from mistakes without significant repercussions. These small experiments help you build confidence and competence as you gradually expand on your ideas.

In iterative learning, constant feedback is key. By rolling out ideas to small groups, you gather actionable insights for the next version of your product or strategy. Throughout this process, you're forming new neural pathways that teach you how to release half-baked ideas, manage risk, quiet your ego, and more.

## In iterative learning, constant feedback is key.

Building these traits requires deep changes in habitual behaviors and thought patterns, which can be challenging and require consistent, deliberate practice. Habits form when repeated behaviors become automatic responses, so it's crucial to consciously practice these new skills daily. Take a pause before responding to difficult situations, keep your vision in mind when making decisions, and weigh new opportunities against the goals you're working toward. Starting with small, manageable changes can help build confidence. Ideally, you should begin with a smaller pivot in one department or aspect of your business—or perhaps just internal work on yourself. As these small changes become habitual, they lay the groundwork for larger behavioral shifts.

Growth isn't just about trial and error; it's also about staying open to new ideas, techniques, and mindsets. The more you practice, the faster and more confidently you'll pivot and innovate. Having a support system in place greatly enhances habit formation. It can provide both encouragement and accountability, which are essential for maintaining new habits over time.

## Personal and professional growth are deeply interconnected.

## CONCLUSION

The skills and traits you develop as an entrepreneur extend far beyond the business realm; they transform how you approach every aspect of life. Personal and professional growth are deeply interconnected: improving business performance often leads to profound personal development. For many business owners, the line between personal and professional growth becomes blurred. The resilience, strategic thinking, and problem-solving abilities honed in your business naturally carry over into your personal life, equipping you to better navigate challenges and make important decisions in all areas. For instance, the resilience we've cultivated through entrepreneurship helped us adapt swiftly during unexpected changes on our trip to Italy. Similarly, the empathy and leadership skills you refine while managing a team enhance your relationships and interactions in your community.

Having owned a staffing business for over a decade while maintaining the same management staff throughout, we've seen firsthand how much personal growth comes with leadership. We can confidently say that we show up differently as parents, friends, and partners because of the skills we've developed in managing employees. The lessons learned in business don't just make you a better entrepreneur—they make you a better person.

This integration suggests that the growth of a business owner is holistic—touching and enhancing every facet of life. The patience learned through iterative business processes can result in more thoughtful parenting or deeper partnerships. The courage to embrace risks and innovate in your business can inspire personal ventures, igniting passions and creating balance beyond work. The parallels between business and life become more pronounced as you realize that growth in one area amplifies progress in the other.

> ## The growth of a business owner is holistic—touching and enhancing every facet of life.

We cannot express how significantly business has impacted our personal lives. It has challenged and stretched us in ways that are likely only rivaled by parenting. In fact, much like raising children, running a business requires constant attention, adaptability, and a willingness to evolve. Both demand an unwavering commitment, often pushing you beyond your perceived limits. For example, navigating personal challenges, like unexpected family health issues or the emotional strains of balancing work and life while raising children, mirrors the unpredictability of the business world. In those moments, the resilience and problem-solving skills we honed in our business life helped us confront these personal challenges with more grace and strategic thinking.

But it has also allowed us to showcase who we are as people and what we are capable of when we step up to the challenge. Though financial success is nice and has allowed us to have things we have dreamed about, money can be spent and lost. It was the personal growth we experienced—the resilience we developed to bounce back from setbacks, the discipline we gained to make tough decisions, and the empathy we cultivated through managing a team—that had the greatest impact on our personal lives. These traits improved our relationships, strengthened our resolve in hard times, and shaped us into more thoughtful parents, partners, and leaders.

The profound truth is that we have had a larger impact on the many entrepreneurs we have served and the many people whose lives they touch as a result. And that is the most fulfilling thing. To know that we have done it while maintaining our integrity, staying true to who we are, and remaining aligned with our vision for our lives gives us a deep sense of fulfillment—one we want everyone to experience.

Embracing the journey of personal and professional development is transformative. This journey reignites joy and passion in your role as a business owner. But more than that, it infuses your personal life with a deeper sense of purpose and fulfillment. The path of growth, both personal and professional, is not simply a checklist of steps to follow. Instead, it is a dynamic, continuous cycle of development. Each revolution of this cycle deepens your skills, broadens your understanding, and refines your character. Every go-around is essential for truly embodying the changes you seek to make in both yourself and your business.

This ongoing process aligns with the philosophical concept of becoming—an ongoing evolution, never static, always growing. As you integrate your personal and professional growth, you'll find that improvements in one area naturally elevate your performance and satisfaction in the other. This

> **It's not solely about the goals you achieve— it's about who you become in the process.**

synergy not only accelerates your overall development but also makes the journey itself more meaningful and rewarding. It's not solely about the goals you achieve—it's about who you become in the process.

While you will undoubtedly reach milestones and complete specific phases of your journey, the true essence of growth lies in perpetual motion—always evolving, always moving forward. For business owners, embracing this cycle of growth isn't a burden but a life-enhancing pursuit that enriches both their business and personal lives. This journey is profoundly impactful, not just in terms of professional success but in fostering a rich, well-rounded, and fulfilling existence.

As we reflect on everything we've explored throughout this book, it's clear that the journey of aligning action with vision—whether in business or life—is not a linear path, nor one marked by simple milestones. Instead, it's an ongoing process of refinement, adaptation, and growth. Through the Power of the PIVOT, we've uncovered the tools, strategies, and mindset shifts that allow us to navigate these continuous changes with purpose and direction.

All of this is a choice. Just like the decision you made to step into business ownership, you are now at another juncture—a new opportunity to pivot your approach and understanding of how to do business. More specifically, it's about choosing a path that may feel unfamiliar, risky, or even a little intimidating. But it's also a path that excites you, one where you can envision the possibilities and know that the work ahead is worth it.

From the moment we face a critical decision to the ongoing adjustments that define our path, pivoting becomes the foundation for success. As this book draws to a close, the lessons we've explored are not merely abstract concepts but actionable steps designed to help you evolve, both personally and professionally. You can see now that pivoting is a tool, *a how*, to take aligned action. The subtitle of this book actually captures the essence better: how to identify what you want, pursue it with purpose, and strategically align every action and decision with that vision.

Ultimately, the goal of this book is to equip you with the tools and mindset necessary to cultivate a strategic, adaptable approach that permeates every aspect of your life and business. The PIVOT framework offers a clear path toward aligning your actions with your vision, empowering you to lead with intention, respond proactively, and seize opportunities with confidence.

You now see and know a secret that the majority of business owners will never understand and would never have the language to articulate. You recognize what it means to be on defense, playing someone else's game, being constantly pinned against your own endzone, bending to give up three points instead of seven. And more than that, you now know how to get yourself on offense. To build the sandcastle of your dreams, not iterations of other ones you've seen while walking along the beach. Soon enough, others will be marveling at what you have; not that it matters, but certainly it feels good. Because you're playing your own game now.

**➤ All of this is a choice.**

In the ever-changing landscape of business and life, the ability to pivot is the key to not just surviving but thriving. The tools you've gained in these pages aren't merely for navigat-

→ **You're playing your own game now.**

ing immediate challenges—they're for actively shaping the future you desire. Every decision you make, every strategy you implement, and every pivot you embrace will not only address current obstacles but also position you for long-term success and fulfillment.

By leveraging the principles of the PIVOT framework, you now have the foundation to align your actions with your vision, no matter what challenges or opportunities arise. This is the power of the pivot—the ability to transform, evolve, and thrive in the face of change. Now, it's time for you to take these insights and apply them, guiding your business and life toward the success you envision.

# HERE'S WHAT TO DO NEXT

Congratulations on completing *The Power of the PIVOT!* Your journey toward taking aligned action and achieving your vision is just beginning. To continue building on what you've learned, here's what you can do next:

## 1. Access Your Free Resources

Dive deeper with the exclusive resources and tools mentioned throughout this book. Visit p10.co/book to access your free bonuses and start implementing the PIVOT framework with confidence.

## 2. Join Our P10 Mentorship Membership

Looking for answers, ongoing accountability, and a community of like-minded entrepreneurs? Join our P10 Mentorship Membership for direct access to us and a network dedicated to taking aligned action. Get the support you need to turn your vision into reality. Learn more at p10.co/membership.

## 3. Hire Us to Speak

Want to inspire and empower your team or event attendees? Book Alisha, Maurice, or both of us for a speaking engagement tailored to your needs. We'll share our experiences, insights, and actionable strategies to help your audience take aligned action in their personal and professional lives. Email speakers@p10.co to inquire.

### 4. Connect with Us on Social Media

Stay connected and follow our journey as we continue to share insights, tips, and stories. Follow Alisha at **@itsalishamp** and Maurice at **@themauricep**. We'd love to hear from you and see how you're applying the PIVOT framework in your life!

Thank you for reading, and here's to taking aligned action and creating the success and fulfillment you deserve!

# ACKNOWLEDGMENTS

This book is the result of countless hours of intention and effort put into our lives and work. However, it would not have happened without the support of an incredible team. To our editor, Miriam, your support and belief in this project was invaluable. To Jake for showing us that writing a book is more about who you become in the process. To the talented design team and Mikey, we are grateful for your energy and passion in making this book impactful from front to back.

To our families and friends, your trust and belief in us has been a consistent source of inspiration. Thank you to our daughters, Tatum and Sloan, your love and smiles melt the stress of long days away. To our parents, who have always believed in our ability to create something meaningful, we are forever thankful.

We want to thank the mentors and teachers who have shaped our thinking, especially Julie Max and Greg Barnett, who in their own ways taught us the importance of aligning action with vision. Without you, we wouldn't be here today.

A special acknowledgment goes to the entrepreneurs and business owners we've worked with over the years—you've taught us so much, and your stories inspired many of the lessons we share here. This book would not have been possible without you.

## ABOUT THE AUTHORS

Alisha and Maurice Pennington are strategic business advisors and co-founders that have helped over 650 entrepreneurs and 60+ businesses across 30 industries. Alisha is also the founder of ATvantage Athletic Training, a staffing company recognized on the Inc. 5000 list for three consecutive years, where Maurice has served as vice president. They draw on their extensive experience in the staffing and business consulting space to guide entrepreneurs through the challenges of growth, leadership, and strategic planning. Their PIVOT framework empowers business owners to align their work with their life goals, ensuring sustainable success without sacrificing personal fulfillment. When Alisha isn't developing new business models and Maurice isn't pursuing his passion for home design, they're focused on raising their two daughters, enjoying sports and entertainment, and traveling.

www.ingramcontent.com/pod-product-compliance
Lightning Source LLC
Chambersburg PA
CBHW020447130626
46549CB00001B/335